D0723248

Hollywood OF THE
ROCKIES

Hollywood OF THE
ROCKIES

COLORADO, THE WEST & AMERICA'S
FILM PIONEERS

MICHAEL J. SPENCER

Charleston | London

THE
History
PRESS

Published by The History Press
Charleston, SC 29403
www.historypress.net

Front cover, clockwise from left: Margaret Herrick Library, Academy of Motion Picture Arts and
Sciences; Museum of the City of New York / Art Resource, New York; Margaret Herrick
Library, Academy of Motion Picture Arts and Sciences; History Colorado.
Back cover, clockwise from left: Niles Essanay Silent Film Museum; History Colorado; Denver
Public Library, Western History Department.

First published 2013

Manufactured in the United States

ISBN 978.1.60949.743.9

Library of Congress CIP data applied for.

Contents

Acknowledgements

They say that film is a collaborative art. In many ways, it's the same with a book: the author gets a lot of help from a lot of sources. So, I'd like to take the time here to give a big thanks to the people and the institutions that helped me put this book together and made their resources available to me.

First, of course, is Rocky Mountain PBS, where my original television documentary began. And for particular help in reassembling some of my notes from that time, I'd like to acknowledge Donna Sanford and Diane Ceraficci. The program was originally a part of the Rocky Mountain Legacy series, executive produced by Sherry Niermann.

I'm truly indebted to Janet Lorenz of the Margaret Herrick Library at the Academy of Motion Picture Arts and Sciences. Starting from years ago with the documentary, she has been able to track down both obscure and not-so-obscure images and information with equal ease.

Coi Drummond-Gehrig and Bruce Hanson with the Denver Public Library, Western History Collection, helped to corral the items in their vast and wonderful collection, which is superbly managed by Jim Kroll.

I received tireless assistance from Sarah Gilmor at History Colorado, especially in helping to track down images and information that I, at first, thought might be impossible to find.

David Emrich is the dean of Colorado film history. He's researched the topic for years, and his own private collection is extensive. He acted as consultant for the television documentary.

David Kiehn's knowledge and research is unfathomable. He's also the historian of the Niles Essanay Silent Film Museum in Niles, California, devoted to silent film in general and Essanay films in particular. He's the go-to source for all things Gilbert Anderson.

Thanks to the Columbia University Center for Oral History for supplying the transcript of conversations held with Gilbert Anderson in 1958.

And finally, where would I be without Steve Hansen? I'm indebted to you, not just as a researcher but also as a friend for life.

A Note on the Book's Organization

The book is divided into three parts, and each has a separate story. I tell you this so you won't get lost and wander around the pages, unsure where you're going.

Part I is the story of the movies in Colorado's Rocky Mountains during the early years of the film industry. In fact, you could consider that this part covers the entire topic. The other parts are devoted to supplementary information. Part II gives some more detailed background to the subject for those whose curiosity warrants it. Part III gives a few hints on where to view some of these movies today.

PART I

EXPLORERS OF THE FILM FRONTIER

This is a book about an age of filmmaking that most people don't even know existed. It's a book about a group of people that, almost by accident, pulled movies out of the realm of novelty and into the realm of business—and ultimately into the realm of art.

These days, people think of early cinema—if they think of it at all—as the luminous outpouring of Hollywood's "Golden Age" of the 1930s or '40s. A few hardy fans of silent film will reminisce about the soundless glories of the 1920s. The more daring will extend their applause back into the 1910s. So it might come as a surprise to find that there was a fierce industry flourishing long before all of that. The movie business was already thriving before Charlie Chaplin first shambled in front of a camera or Douglas Fairbanks leaped onto the screen or Mary Pickford sighed demurely on film.

This is the story of those early days—more particularly, a specific part of those days: a part lying west of New York but east of California, in the Rocky Mountains of Colorado. It's a tale of the role that the West played in shaping the American film industry. Of course, there were many early film pioneers who didn't film in the West, but there were many who did. And this is their story.

All things seem to change a little when they pass through Colorado. It's a crossroads of sorts, where people and ideas come together, collide, merge, become inspired, create some new spark and pop out the other end completely changed animals. Even the weather becomes more than the weather; this is where the winds and breezes moving across the country hit the mountains and transform themselves into giant storms and towering thunderheads or dissipate into gentle zephyrs. Either way, they've been changed.

And so it was that in the early twentieth century, the area served as a sort of incubator for ideas that were traveling through the country and would eventually move on and reach their zenith in what would become the film capital known as Hollywood. Ultimately, it was more than the scenery that affected the filmmakers, these newcomers to the Front Range of the Colorado Rockies—it was an indefinable something in the very air.

It was, however, the landscape that brought them there in the first place. Colorado rather lucked out with its gorgeous, natural scenery, perfect for the country's (and the world's) growing infatuation with the West. The most important star of these films wasn't in the cast; rather, it was the Colorado West itself. It helped create the western, a genre that remained a staple of American films for decades. And though the western film is certainly not the box office draw it once was, its spirit still inhabits the soul not only of American films but international films as well.

More importantly, it led moving pictures to realize what they really are by revealing their quality of "locationness"—the authenticity of place that lifts films from the burden of merely documenting staged performances. Landscape and setting became just as significant as character and plot (and, importantly to the early film entrepreneurs, made for significant box office profits as well). It began when movies discovered the vast expanse of open space and embraced the mythos of the West.

To be sure, Colorado wasn't the only western state to play host to the pioneering filmmakers. Wyoming, Montana, Oklahoma, Arizona and New Mexico are just a few of the other states that lent their scenery to the growing film industry. But Colorado had just about the best back lot imaginable, and those early filmmakers used it to its best advantage.

Watching these old films today, frankly, they look pretty beat up. A lot of this, of course, is simply the result of age—the scratchy, bouncing images rendered unsteady because of overrunning through a projector. But even looking beyond that, there's definitely a certain primitivism to these films. The action is conspicuously staged, and the characters are awkwardly posed for benefit of the completely static camera position: a close approximation of the best seat in a live theater—front row, center. But if you look at these films through different, un-modern eyes, you see that they captured a raw naturalism, a genuineness of human interaction that is often lacking in present-day films. Perhaps we've all become too enamored of today's sophisticated production values.

The people who made those early films lived full and rich lives and gave considerable thought as to how to depict their subjects. Yet we see only transient moments of their lives briefly passing by, one frame at a time. It's easy to engage in dorm room philosophy here, rhapsodizing on the transience of life and personality, how these filmmakers of the past are really not so different from us. And that's true. But mostly they were just having a great time making a living and enjoying themselves in a business they loved.

Toward the end of his life, one of these pioneers, William Selig, reflected back on the early days of filmmaking. "[T]here is a bigger, more human story in the little tragedies and comedies of real life which marked each successive step of our progress in the early days."

This, then, is that human story that lies within the "little tragedies and comedies" of America's film pioneers.

Prelude to the West

We all know the happy ending: Hollywood becomes the film capital of the world, stars bask in the California surf and the West Coast turns into something a little more than just a geographic location. That's the Hollywood story, and it's mostly true, but it leaves out something very important: the beginning.

What happened before the opening credits of that movie spectacle we call "Hollywood"? The whole business actually began before Hollywood even existed, half a world away, in what at the time was considered the much more civilized part of the world: Europe and the East Coast—more specifically Paris and New York. But as the American film industry began to grow and set out on its inexorable journey toward California, it made a somewhat brief but eventful stay in the Rocky Mountains of Colorado and created a temporary "Hollywood of the Rockies."

But all this was yet to come, way back in 1895, when the Lumière brothers premiered the first motion picture projector, the cinématographe, to an astonished audience at the Grande Café in Paris. The Lumière brothers, Auguste and Louis, were heirs to their father's photographic business and had been impressed by a small peep show version of moving images. They developed a method to project those tiny pictures onto a giant screen.

Moving pictures, as big as life, were something that had never been seen before. The brothers arranged for a few private screenings before their official debut, and people were already talking about the magic, life-sized moving images. As it happened, celebrated Russian author Maxim Gorky was among the first to view these projected images, and his comments give us a sense of the revelation that first greeted these images:

> *A beam of electric light is projected on a large screen, mounted in a dark room. And a photograph appears on the cloth screen. We see a street in Paris. The picture shows carriages, children, pedestrians: frozen into immobility, trees covered with leaves. All of these are still. And suddenly there is a sound somewhere, the picture shivers, you don't believe your eyes. The carriages are moving straight at you, the pedestrians are walking, the children are playing with a dog. Leaves are fluttering on the trees, and bicyclists roll along. And suddenly it disappears. Your eyes see a plain piece of white cloth in a wide black frame, and it seems as if nothing had been there. You feel that you have imagined something that you had just seen with your own eyes—and that's all. You feel indefinably awestruck.*

The Lumière brothers made a string of short films that they exhibited over the next few years before famously, and prematurely, stating that "the cinema is an invention without any future," abandoning it to the world. There were others who had more faith in the future of films.

Of course, in order for anything to succeed in the modern world, it has to be readily available for commercial exploitation. And there was no one who appreciated this better than America's premier entrepreneur-inventor, Thomas Edison. Edison is one of those people who really needs no introduction, but just to set the stage, let me give you a little background. By the 1890s, Edison was already practically a mythical figure—many of those myths being of his own devising. He had already introduced the world to the incandescent light bulb, the phonograph record and the electrical grid, and there were countless other patents registered in his name (a record 1,093 in his lifetime). He practically created the world as we know it, or at least a good part of it. He was Steve Jobs, Bill Gates, Mark Zuckerberg and Walt Disney all rolled into one. And although he didn't personally invent the motion picture projector, he's forever linked in our minds as the man who created the movies. And how that happened has more to do with commerce than creativity.

Edison was already at the forefront of moving picture technology with his Kinetoscope—not a projector but rather a peep show device designed for individual viewing of moving images. Kinetoscopes were small viewing boxes set up in what were known as Kinetoscope Parlors; patrons would pay a nickel and look through a peephole to view a scene that ran about twenty

The appropriately named Lumière brothers, Auguste (left) and Louis (right), didn't invent moving pictures, but they were the first to successfully project them onto a screen. Their father attended a demonstration of Edison's Kinetoscope peep show viewer, designed for individual use. He admonished the brothers to "get that image out of the box." They did and made cinema history, releasing the moving images onto the screen. The location was the Grande Café in Paris, now the site of the Hotel Scribe, which operates a restaurant called Le Café Lumière. *Courtesy Margaret Herrick Library, Academy of Motion Picture Arts and Sciences.*

"In appearance, manner and language he reminds you of the best type of the great Middle West, of a prosperous, philosophical farmer, or the shrewd and kindly president of a rural bank." So said *The Moving Picture World* of Thomas Edison in 1914. He had already revolutionized the day-to-day landscape of America with his electric light bulb, phonograph player, moving pictures and a host of other inventions. *Courtesy Museum of the City of New York / Art Resource, New York.*

seconds. They would see images of people sneezing, smoking a pipe, dancing and other basic activities. Sounds pretty simple, but to people in 1894, it was a little bit of magic and worth every penny. (It was Edison's Kinetoscope that had inspired the Lumière brothers to create their cinématographe machine.)

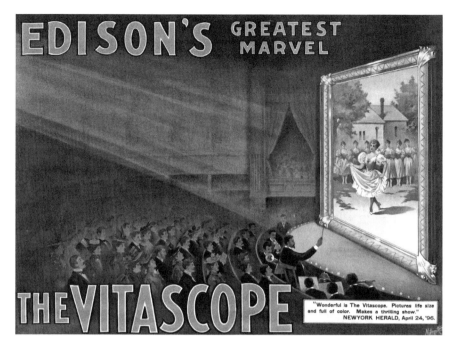

Edison's Vitascope brought movies to a mass audience. The poster advertises that the films are "full of color." This was accomplished by tinting the film by hand, either frame by frame or with a stencil. Note the oversized gilt picture frame around the screen, a device used to emphasize the fact that these were moving "pictures." *Courtesy Library of Congress, Prints and Photographs Division.*

However, in 1895, after a single year of booming business, the novelty was already wearing off, and so was the revenue stream. Edison was on the verge of abandoning the business entirely when he was approached by Thomas Armat, an inventor who had perfected a new twist on the moving picture novelty—projecting images onto a screen. Edison was all for it. He had been tinkering with various projection devices himself but had more or less shelved the project as return on costs seemed to be diminishing.

We all know how important branding is. Well, Armat and Edison did too. They knew that anything with the name "Edison" attached to it would sell better than the name Armat had previously been using, Phantoscope (although frankly, anything would be a step up from that). In a marketing deal that would make Bill Gates envious, Edison's company bought the patent and began manufacturing the projector with the much more marketable Edison name attached. Everyone looked forward to hefty profits. And they weren't disappointed.

So, on April 23, 1896, the Edison Vitascope premiered at Koster and Bial's Music Hall, New York's biggest vaudeville theater (Macy's now stands on this spot in Herald Square). It was announced with one of the typically extravagant newspaper accounts that the not-so-modest Edison graciously accepted: "EDISON'S LATEST INVENTION. With It He Will Show Us a Railroad Wreck and the Pope Saying Mass. The vitascope, Thomas A. Edison's perfection of the idea that caused the world to marvel when he produced the kinetoscope, has been dividing triumph…at Koster & Bial's since Thursday night, and 'the Wizard of Menlo Park' promises that before many days he will need an entire stage for the screen on which his latest invention shows life and color."

The presentation started with dancing girls, a surefire crowd pleaser. "In Gauzy Silks They Smirk and Pirouette at Wizard Edison's Command. Perfect Reproduction of Noted Feminine Figures and Their Every Movement." But even in sophisticated New York, the dancing girls weren't the hit of the evening. The clip that really got people leaping up out of their seats was a simple sixty-second shot of the ocean, with "the waves tumbling in on a beach and about a stone pier that caused the spectators to cheer and to marvel most of all. Big rollers broke on the beach, foam flew high, and weakened waters poured far up the beach. Then great combers arose and pushed each other shoreward, one mounting above the other, until they seemed to fall with mighty force and all together on the shifty sand, whose yellow, receding motion could be plainly seen."

The Vitascope was a sensation, and within months, competing vaudeville theaters were adding motion picture acts to their variety shows. These films were no longer than sixty seconds each and were presented as little more than one more act in an evening's variety show lineup, usually in groups of five. So, for example, between the baggy-pants comedian and the charming contralto, you might see a few minutes of President McKinley addressing a crowd, Chinese dancers or merely a train arriving at a station—single-shot films, barely one minute in length.

To really understand the impact that moving pictures had on people at the turn of that century, you have to travel back there in your mind and forget about everything you know about movies. Forget about sound, forget about stars and forget about dramas, epics, comedies and art films. Forget what happened to movies as they matured in the twentieth century. All you know is that there's a two-dimensional image in front of you that's moving. And that's never happened before. Nobody had any idea whatsoever of the direction this little novelty was destined to take, least of all Thomas

A good old-fashioned family film (literally), *Baby's Breakfast (Repas de bébé)* featured Auguste Lumière, his wife and his child in a simple domestic scene. The running time was about fifty seconds, and it was shown with nine other short films in the first commercial screening of a moving picture program. *Courtesy (Cat. N°88), Louis Lumière, Lyon, 1895,* © *Association Frères Lumière.*

Edison himself. He later recalled, "Well, at first we used to turn out films of an average length of about two hundred feet and the subjects were all scenic. The idea to utilize the invention for the purposes of the drama came much later."

In those formative years, audiences were thrilled just to see a moving image, and simple scenes of everyday life held a great fascination for those pre-blockbuster audiences. Think about those early days of YouTube, when people posted video of their kids falling off the roof, and "Charlie bit my finger" became the most viewed video of all time. The Lumière films included *Baby's Breakfast, Workers Leaving the Lumière Factory* and (my favorite) *The Gardener, or the Bad Boy and the Hose*, a laugh-riot of a film wherein a gardener's assistant steps on a watering hose to keep the water from coming out, until the gardener looks directly into the nozzle. Then—*whoosh*—right in the face! As a catalogue described it, "It ends in a thorough wetting for both, and the total defeat of the mischievous urchin." Real corker stuff, eh?

And there were other ways to wow a crowd. One of the more popular Edison films, *The Kiss*, was described in film catalogues as, "An osculatory performance…The most popular subject ever shown. They get *ready* to Kiss, *begin* to Kiss, and Kiss and Kiss and Kiss in a way that brings down the house."

Filmmakers became more adventuresome and more mobile and began shooting scenes from around the world. At a time when people could barely afford a trip to the next county, a few cents could take them on a journey across the globe at the movies. Even an anonymous clerk in a Harlem cigar store could book passage to foreign locales: "I enjoy these shows for they continually introduce me to new places and new people. If I ever go to Berlin or Paris I will know what the places look like. I have seen…gold mined…in Alaska, and diamonds dug in South Africa."

So, as early as 1898, still in the formative years of the motion picture business, the American West began making guest appearances on the silver screen. Colorado was the star of *Horticultural Floats*, a film showing a parade in the Festival of Mountain and Plain in Denver, Colorado. The film catalogue extolled, "These contain the prominent people of the city in costume for the occasion. The fashionable equipages are garlanded with flowers."

Or how about an authentic taste of the real West with *Procession of Mounted Indians and Cowboys*? This little film "[s]hows the grand-stand, corner of Broadway and Colfax avenue, with Indian braves and squaws passing; also rough cowboys on half-tamed bronchos." In those days, of course, all cowboys were rough cowboys.

But in these early days, movie producers had no qualms about shooting staged events if it was cheaper. So, in 1899, we have an early western-themed motion picture called *A Cripple Creek Barroom*, filmed to capitalize on the name of the still booming Colorado mining town. I'll lay out the scenario for you. We see the interior of a bar in Cripple Creek, a gold camp that was still thought of as a lawless community. A group of miners is playing poker, a fight ensues and the barmaid (played by a man) knocks heads together to stop the brawling. She also makes use of a seltzer bottle—just to add some authenticity, I suppose. The whole thing was shot, of course, in Edison's New Jersey studio. Audiences didn't seem to mind. To them, it was a filmed version of a staged event.

And the real miracle for us is that we're still able to view these films today. Most of them, shot well over one hundred years ago, have long since

Who doesn't love a parade? Audiences around the world got their first glimpse of cowboys and Indians in their natural habitat in such films as *Horticultural Floats*, shot at the Festival of Mountain and Plain in Denver, Colorado, in 1896. The only way for us to see the film today is by looking at the blurry, vestigial copy of it in the Paper Print Collection of the Library of Congress. Kemp R. Niver, the first curator of this collection, noted, "Until the completion of the paper-print conversion program, one would never have known of the existence of films of many long-forgotten and possibly never-again-recalled public occasions." *Courtesy Library of Congress, Paper Print Collection.*

disintegrated to dust, yet we're still able to watch them. And the reason for that is an interesting story in its own right. It came about through an accident of the copyright system. At the time, there was absolutely no precedent for copyrighting moving images. The need simply hadn't existed until then, and nobody really knew how to do it. So, in order to copyright their motion pictures, these filmmakers would literally unroll the entire length of their completed films and lay them flat on a strip of photo printing paper as long and as wide as the original film. They'd expose the image and end up with a paper print of the film. It wasn't a great reproduction—in fact, it looked something like a bad Xerox copy. But they could then copyright it as a graphic work of art. Sounds extreme, but that's the only way that we have

A frame from *A Cripple Creek Barroom*. Painted backdrops and hillbilly props didn't lend much to the authenticity of the film, but it all still made for a pretty lively forty-five seconds of screen time. *Courtesy Cripple Creek District Museum.*

some of these films today, and hundreds of them are now available in the Paper Print Collection at the U.S. Library of Congress.

What to us is a cherished glimpse into the world of the past was to the folks of the 1890s an amusing novelty. But as the decade wore on, that novelty of moving pictures started to wear thin, and audiences began to dwindle. So, filmmakers hit on the formula that's been their standby ever since: action! With the outbreak of the Spanish-American War in 1898, motion pictures found a subject that would bring audiences back to the theater. And movie producers couldn't have been more ecstatic. After one of the first presentations of war films at a New York vaudeville theater, Albert Smith, a Vitagraph producer, was thrilled with the audience's response. "That night at Pastor's the audience, enthralled with the idea of a war with Spain, saw their boys marching for the first time on any screen. They broke into a

In the days before powerful indoor studio lighting was practical, film companies shot everything out of doors—even interior scenes. This engraving from a *Scientific American* magazine of 1897 shows just how it's done using a rooftop studio. The camera is in the corrugated shed on the left. It can travel on a track to bring it closer to or farther from the stage. The entire structure rotates on a circular track in order to catch full sunlight any time of the day. *Author's collection.*

thunderous storm of shouting and foot stamping. Hats and coats filled the air. Never had Pastor's witnessed such a night."

When our boys went to war, the movies went with them, more or less. Though cameras would on occasion actually accompany the troops to Cuba, usually the battle scenes were dramatizations staged in New York or New Jersey. But the public ate it up, so much so that for a while, the generic name for movies became the "wargraph."

As the war wound down, other filmmakers, working outside the boundaries of the East Coast film establishment, began acting on a vision for the potential of this infant industry and launched a direct competition with Edison and the old guard of the movie business. And it was one of this new breed, an itinerate magician out of Chicago, who would bring filmmaking to the Rocky Mountains.

Hopping on the Movie Bandwagon

The life of a traveling vaudeville entertainer was beginning to wear thin for Colonel Selig. Oh sure, life on the stage can seem so romantically picaresque at the start of the venture, but then the grueling insecurity of it all kicks in.

William Selig (pronounced *see*-lig) was possibly the most interesting and significant film pioneer you've never heard of. He looked a little like the character of Professor Marvel in *The Wizard of Oz* and lived the life that you'd imagine that character would have lived—magician, itinerate entertainer, salesman. He was no more an actual colonel than was Colonel Sanders, the creator of Kentucky Fried Chicken, but the title fit him grandly. Born in 1864 the second generation of Bohemian and Prussian immigrants, he learned magic as a teen in Chicago and was good enough that he was able to eke out a living on the variety circuit. Due to poor health, he traveled westward through Colorado and California to take in the clear air of the West, getting odd jobs here and there and even for a time managing a health resort in northern California (ironically called Chicago Park). But the convalescent life was not for him, and as soon as his health returned, he was back on the road, touring up and down the coast, sometimes performing in dime museums, sometimes managing minstrel shows and sometimes leading wagon shows across the backcountry. Dog acts, olios, musical shticks. Yes, it was time to go home.

And it was while he was trying to work his way back to Chicago that it happened. In the autumn of 1895 in Dallas, William Selig first laid eyes on the machine that would transform his life forever. He wandered into a

Colonel Selig looking quite dapper. The onetime magician and minstrel show impresario filled the role of showman with a cheerful panache. *Courtesy Margaret Herrick Library, Academy of Motion Picture Arts and Sciences.*

Kinetoscope Parlor and beheld the flickering, dreamlike movement of the little figures inside the box—the miniature dancers, the diminutive boxers, the tiny men sneezing. Like many others, he immediately imagined the creative and monetary potential to be had in projecting the images on a screen for large audiences.

From that point on, he had a single vision, both as a showman and as a businessman: to create a moving picture projection machine. And once back in Chicago, he rented a small workshop and began drawing up designs for his own projection device. In the tried-and-true method of entrepreneurs, he supported himself with various day (and sometimes night) jobs and opened a small photography business that shot large panoramic murals for railroad companies. That was going to come in handy for him later. As it happened, at about this time, the Lumière cinématographe was beginning to make its way across the United States, from vaudeville house to vaudeville house, and one eventually found its way to the Schiller Theatre in Chicago. Selig managed to salvage a few scraps of film from the theater to use as a pattern. It was simple, right? You had the film; just design a machine to go around it.

Although handy with tools and an avid tinkerer, Selig was more showman than inventor, and the successful design of a motion picture projector eluded him. And he might never have made it into the world of film production if not for an incredible stroke of good luck.

In order to fine-tune the manufacture of his projector, he sought the assistance of a mechanic in the Union Model Works of Chicago. As fate would have it, this mechanic had already had his own close encounter with a projection machine. It seems that a few months earlier, the mechanic had been approached by a mysterious stranger who wanted him to duplicate a small part that he possessed from some unnamed machine. Of course, making models is what Union Model Works did for a living, so our mechanic made a working drawing and duplicated the part for the stranger. And that was that.

But the next day, the stranger brought in another part for duplication as well. Our mechanic dutifully made a drawing and duplicated the part. This went on for quite some time until it became apparent that the machine being duplicated, part by part, was none other than the Lumière cinématographe. The stranger (who had a French accent, I might add) eventually ended up with all the pieces of his unassembled machine and left—no one knows where. The mechanic kept the set of drawings.

Into this situation stepped Colonel Selig, with his own drawings for a not quite successful projection machine. It didn't take him long to spot the cinématographe drawings and realize the situation (and his own good fortune in it). With some of the gaps in his design now clarified, he entered into a partnership with the mechanic and, in 1896, unveiled to the world his own variation of a motion picture projector, which he dramatically (and not very humbly) called the Selig Polyscope.

By now, of course, everyone was coming up with their own versions of a motion picture projector. As one commentator later observed, it seemed that around every corner there was "some little man with a moving picture camera of his very own, constructed from a cigar box, some spare parts from a plow, and pieces of his grandmother's sewing machine." There was the Centograph, the Panoramographe, the Cineograph, the Animotiscope and the Kalatechnoscope. So really, the name Polyscope wasn't that much of a stretch—and probably a good deal easier to pronounce than the others.

Selig opened a small business, which he called the Selig Polyscope Company, supplying films and projectors to local vaudeville houses and other places of amusement. He started with simple films of local scenes: people walking on well-known Chicago streets, dogs chasing people, the Chicago stockyards and the neighborhood fire brigades—the fire brigades were very important to early filmmakers. As the Colonel later remembered, "The movies then consisted of nothing longer than fifty foot strips—one scene, usually of a fire department in active eruption or something else depicting some every day occurrence in which action dominated."

Another big hit of his was a short scenario involving a tramp stealing a pie from a window ledge. A bulldog spots him and gives chase, biting him on the seat of his pants as he's about to climb over a fence. The big denouement comes as the fence collapses under the weight of the tramp—a joke not written in the script but rather was one of those unintended happy accidents that worked. "That picture was more than a sensation," Selig recalled. "It was a riot." To those of you who think that it might not play as well to a modern audience, let me remind you of any of the typical sight gags from the perennially popular *Scooby-Doo* cartoons.

Things would have been rosy indeed if it weren't for the emergence of a series of legal proceedings that came to be known as the Motion Picture Patent Wars. Selig and just about all of the other film pioneers were being sued by Thomas Edison for infringement on his motion picture projection patents. Other names included on the hit list were the Biograph Company, the Vitagraph Company, Georges Méliès, Pathé and others.

Edison saw them as nothing more than common outlaws trying to horn in on his business and viewed the whole matter as justifiable and moral. Much later in life, he reminisced about his "fight with the pirates; that always is a matter of course. We had to fight them in the courts and our expenses were enormous." However, Colonel Selig took the whole matter a little more

Inside the Selig Polyscope camera. Technology was a lot different in the late 1890s, when this motion picture camera was one of many at the center of a patents war. The top spool is feeding the bottom spool through the film gate on the right. It was hand-cranked. *Courtesy History Colorado.*

personally and felt that "Mr. Edison is about to put me out of business with an injunction on patents."

The patent wars slogged on for years, with suits and countersuits dragging filmmakers through the courts. But like most entrepreneurs, Selig was resilient and persevered through the storm. It wasn't long before he realized the potential of larger markets—something that could be sold to theaters across the country, beyond the Chicago area. And then he remembered his days in the sun-drenched West. "They all had a lot of trouble with the light back around Chicago and New York. [Out West] I had noticed that the light was softer and the results better. Then there was the advantage of fine weather most of the year, an advantage we certainly did not enjoy in the east."

So, he set his filmic sights back to Colorado, where, by 1902, he had hooked up with an old friend he knew from the early days of his photographic business preparing large panoramics for the railroads—a Colorado booster who in some ways out-marveled Professor Marvel himself.

If it was new, if it was modern, Harry "Buck" Buckwalter wanted to be a part of it. A newspaper photographer and *bon vivant*, Buckwalter dove in head first to the intellectual curiosity of the age. A partial list of his accomplishments includes the invention of a Detectophone (which was exactly what it sounds like: a device for listening through walls that was used by the U.S. Secret Service); the invention of something he called an Air Washing Machine, which employed "reverse ventilation" to circulate and clean the air; the first X-ray pictures in the West; wireless transmission; and (more prosaically) the invention of a high-speed shutter for the camera. And by the early 1900s, his new passion was for motion picture photography.

As far as Buckwalter was concerned, Colorado was the only place any sensible person would really want to live. He told people, "There is too much sunshine in this state to waste time on the clouds." In the 1880s, at the green age of sixteen, he had pulled up stakes and left the family home in Reading, Pennsylvania, deciding to strike out on his own in his chosen land of opportunity: the western frontier of Colorado. He soon became a leading player in advancing the mythos of the West.

Buckwalter, like Selig, was an extravagant showman, and he enjoyed promoting Colorado and himself through motion pictures. In fact, Buckwalter was so keen on boosting Colorado that he cooked up a particularly imaginative publicity stunt to lure visitors to the state. A misconception about Colorado (then and now) was that the entire state shut down for most of the winter due to constant blizzard conditions. Buckwalter decided that he would disprove those stories by daring to film during that notorious winter month of January. He decided to set up his "picture machine" on the front end of the Denver Seventeenth Street trolley car and shoot as the car made its way down the street.

It was quite the production. Denver's tramway superintendent decided to personally drive the car, and several city and state representatives were designated official passengers. Arrangements were made to have the local transportation company fill the streets with coaches, "and have them loaded with pretty girls dressed in light colored finery. Other swell traps are also expected, and these, with the waving of hats and handkerchiefs, will make a very lively scene as the car passes." Indeed.

The day arrived, sunny and dazzling, and as the trolley took off from Union Station, a cannon was fired to signal people down the line to be ready.

Harry "Buck" Buckwalter never missed a chance to try something new and marvelous. What could be more interesting than aerial photography? *Courtesy History Colorado.*

With all the preparation and cross-checking, even nature had to cooperate. The *Denver Times* reported, "It was not necessary for orders to be given to dispense with overcoats. Old Sol had done that earlier in the day. As the car

Buckwalter had to withstand a caricatured countdown to his "winter in Denver" shoot.
You're not really a celebrity unless someone makes a cartoon of you in the local newspaper.
Courtesy History Colorado.

sped down Seventeenth street cheers arose from the crowds, handkerchiefs were waved frantically, and one man, in the exuberance of his spirits, discharged a volley from his revolver." Buckwalter got it all in one take.

Within days, Buckwalter's little epic, *Midwinter Scenes in Denver*, was playing to packed houses across the country. Denver's sunny disposition was made all the more amazing because of vigorous blizzard conditions that hit the eastern seaboard at the time. Of course, a cold snap also engulfed Denver within a few days of the shoot, but that'll be our little secret.

And who acted as distributor for Buckwalter's epic? None other than Colonel Selig. Selig and other film pioneers were quickly catching on to the public's growing appetite for remote locales. There was nothing like the mythic frontier to bring eastern audiences to the theater. Unlike Edison, Colonel Selig himself actually traveled to the open spaces of the wild and woolly West to supervise production of his films. And he brought with him a seasoned Polyscope cameraman, Thomas Nash, to bring Harry Buckwalter up to speed on the nuances of the camera.

BUCK READY TO START HIS PICTURE MACHINE

This rather ragged newspaper photo is all we have left of Buck's celebrated *Midwinter Scenes in Denver*, shot from a moving trolley. The *Denver Times* reported, "Away dashed the car at the speed of an express train. It swayed from side to side but Mr. Buckwalter, by clinging to a hand rail, stood by his camera and fed in the long roll of film." *Courtesy History Colorado.*

Buckwalter, ever the perfectionist, spent long hours studying the unique lighting conditions involved in shooting in the rarified atmosphere of Colorado. When he and Selig got together, these two boosters cooked up some screen magic all their own. As early as 1902, the Selig Polyscope Company's catalogue presented an entire *Special Supplement of Colorado Films*, proclaiming that "all will cheerfully pay liberally to see pictures of this strange land of

Buckwalter takes part in filming a stagecoach. The Selig catalogue of 1902 describes the results: "A gay tally-ho party coming down the narrow trail bordering the Grand river in the canyon a few miles above Glenwood Springs. The horses saw the moving picture machine and started to gallop. The bunch of pretty girls grew excited and suddenly stopped waving handkerchiefs, using both hands to hold on." *Courtesy History Colorado.*

sunshine and beauty, of gold and precious stones. No community in the United States is too small to give ample returns for a show on this subject. The very name of Colorado will attract hundreds, yes, thousands and the exhibitor first on the spot will reap a golden harvest."

The lengths "Buck" Buckwalter went through for the perfect shot were truly phenomenal (and Selig, too, for he would sometimes accompany the camera crews on their ventures)—on one occasion dangling in the air from a hot air balloon and on multiple occasions hanging on to the fronts of railcars pushed by engines across mountainous tracks at speeds "of nearly or quite seventy miles an hour. The wind cut their faces and hands like a knife. Blood flowed from their ears and noses when the engine came to a stop." And in another case, while filming Hell Gate (referred to as the most "scaly" piece of railroad in America), "[t]he experience was so dangerous that it will never

The cover page to a Selig Polyscope catalogue from 1903. What more can be said? *Courtesy Library of Congress, Silent Films Catalogues.*

Putting the camera on a handcar was all in a day's work for camera crews eager to find an unexpected view of the mountains. *Courtesy History Colorado.*

again be attempted for had there been a single hitch the entire 'train' would have been pitched to the bottom of the cliff far below."

But as with modern-day photogs, the shots were worth it—including such footage as a panorama of the Royal Gorge, speeding down Ute Pass by rail, ascending the summit of Pikes Peak and even the occasional runaway

The Georgetown Loop was originally built as a perilous necessity to connect two mining towns, and it immediately became a popular tourist attraction as well. A Colorado landmark and an engineering marvel, the train still operates between the towns of Silver Plume and Georgetown. *Courtesy Denver Public Library, Western History Department.*

stagecoach. But perhaps the most popular scenic was the *Panorama of the Famous Georgetown Loop*. The Loop was considered a significant engineering marvel at the end of the nineteenth century. Railroad surveyors were faced with the dilemma of running a track to connect the mountain towns of Silver Plume and Georgetown, Colorado—a distance of scarcely two miles. The problem was that that distance covered an elevation of one thousand feet up the mountainside. The solution was to put the track through a series of tortuous hairpin curves and bows starting high up in Silver Plume that eventually loop back onto themselves, finally completing an entire circle before arriving down in Georgetown. According to Selig, "The train swings around so many curves the engineer can almost reach the outstretched hands of those in the rear coach."

The clever reader may notice that a lot of these scenics involved the use of railroad cars and railroad travel. This was hardly an accident. The railroads were eager to boost their business and promote their scenic lines. Since both Colonel Selig and "Buck" Buckwalter already had dealings with the railroads, it was a media marriage made in heaven—not unlike the

A fire run was a sure audience draw for all the early filmmakers. Very often, movie exhibitors would stage and film a fire run in the afternoon and have it ready for viewing by the local audiences that night. That's exactly what Buckwalter is doing here. *Courtesy History Colorado.*

product placement deals we see today—and special trains were placed at their service. Buckwalter, ever the honest booster, said, "[T]hat's the kind of 'Seeing America First' advertising that looks good to me."

And Buckwalter paid it back to the people of the community by hosting regular free outdoor screenings of films in Denver's City Park—anticipated events that would draw as many as forty thousand people. They were so popular that they were repeated during the summer months for several years. These shows were made up of a family-friendly mashup of film clips that were representative of the sort of program that would be available in vaudeville theaters and tent shows across the country: scenics, gags and human interest pieces (known at the time as "actualities"). A quick glance at some of the titles shown at these outdoor screenings gives us an idea of what was entertaining people in those days: *Bucking Broncho Contest, Panorama of New York Elevated Railway, Fishing Schooners, Cooling off of the Lovers, Ringling Circus Parade, Street Scene in Jerusalem, Bag-Punching Dog, Mardi Gras Parade at*

New Orleans, Hideous Dance by Indians, Grand Canyon of Arizona, Stage Coach Hold-up and *Babies and Kittens*. Babies and kittens? Holy YouTube! Some things never change.

And wait, what's this? Wouldn't you know it—here's another fire department racing on an emergency run, always the most popular actuality in cities across the nation. It had action, it had heroics and it had "our boys." What exhibitor could pass on a film that "shows the firemen…leaving the engine house; the mad dash out of doors, and the most realistic fire run shown on canvas. Twenty-eight pieces of fire fighting machines madly rushing and plunging down a thoroughfare on the way to the fire…the men putting on their coats and fire hats; the drivers lashing their horses. It is indeed a great and inspiring scene."

With films like these, Selig was booking his programs throughout the United States and beyond, carving a niche to rival Edison himself. But there was change afoot. The world of bag-punching dogs, fire brigades, babies and kittens, bad boy gardeners, baby's breakfasts and tramps being chased by dogs was about to end as a groundbreaking motion picture hit the screens and the industry got ready to take a giant leap in the direction of modern film.

How Far Is West?

W e'd hardly call New Jersey the state where the true West began. But that's where the West of the movies began. It was here where movie producers put together something that would transform the novelty act of the turn of the century into the motion picture industry that we know today, and the movie that started it all was a little 1903 Edison film by Edwin S. Porter called *The Great Train Robbery*. If that sounds like a bit of an overstatement to you, you're probably right. And yet, it's uncannily true.

Much has been written about this film—perhaps too much. But get ready for just a little more because it affects the rest of our story. It has been called the first film to offer a complete narrative, the first to use crosscutting, the first to use camera movement and a host of other firsts—none of which is entirely true. There were other films that had pioneered these techniques, though not in a single film. It has been acknowledged that *The Great Train Robbery* was heavily influenced by other films, most notably *A Daring Daylight Burglary* by British filmmaker Frank Mottershaw and *A Desperate Poaching Affray* by William Haggar. This part is true.

So the question you may be asking is: if it wasn't the first film to do all these things, why does everyone talk about it as if it was such a significant influence? Basically, it wasn't the first film to feature these new production innovations, but it *was* the first film to make a major impact. This is the film that made people sit up and take notice. All these new techniques were finally put together in one film. Even though the audience wasn't specifically analyzing the film with scholarly thoughts like, "Oh, that parallel cut really drew me into the story," or, "That panning shot makes

The western sneaks onto the American movie screen, guns a-blazin'! This frame from *The Great Train Robbery* has become perhaps the most iconic image of the early American film industry. *Courtesy Margaret Herrick Library, Academy of Motion Picture Arts and Sciences.*

me feel like I'm really there," they were viscerally reacting to what we now call film grammar. Was it a hit? Oh, yes. It packed the theaters. It was so popular that it could still open a house as a major presentation in 1905, two years after its initial release.

There was something odd about it, though. The Edison catalogue marketed it as "posed and acted in faithful duplication of the genuine 'Hold Ups' made famous by various outlaw bands in the far West." It was essentially what we would call a western (though that term as such didn't quite exist yet), and the story was set in the West, but it was shot in no wilder a frontier than New Jersey. Nobody involved thought about this anachronism too hard, but there were those in the film community who began wondering if there might be a way to turn a more authentic location to box office advantage.

"Buck" Buckwalter was at the Edison factory for an advanced screening. Being viewed as an expert on western scenes and customs, he had been consulted while the film was being planned and, according to him, had

A frame from *Tracked by Bloodhounds*. See that flag with the diamond shape surreptitiously hanging on the tree behind the tramp? That's Colonel Selig's logo, ever so strategically placed at various points throughout the film as a sort of copyright announcement. Piracy was rampant at the time, and filmmakers would do whatever they could to brand their films. *Courtesy Jones Film and Video Collection, Hamon Arts Library, Southern Methodist University.*

made some suggestions that affected the making of the picture, including some technical advice for staging a pivotal scene in which the robbers throw the train's fireman from the speeding engine.

He was amused by the shooting environment. "People around Orange, N.J. thought a riot was in progress while the film was being made. There was all kinds of shooting in the dance hall and in the neighboring woods. But now the citizens are getting used to unusual things and if a red devil with wings were to fly over the town they would not marvel at it."

Buckwalter, like so many others, was a fan of the film and its technical and narrative accomplishments. But he also was quick to realize the box office potential to be had by including genuine western scenery; he figured that the best location to shoot a western would be—of all places—the West. Of course, as it happened, he and Colonel Selig were already set up to take advantage of the local color from a ready-made western locale: Colorado. And they immediately made the most of the situation.

The Colorado mining town of Cripple Creek was still a hot topic and still thought of as an anarchistic, godforsaken community dangling on the very precipice of the civilized world. You may remember its last starring role as the setting of a lawless barroom a few years back. The Selig Polyscope Company's very next film, melodramatically entitled *Tracked by Bloodhounds or A Lynching at Cripple Creek*, was shot not in New Jersey but in Cripple Creek itself, with "Buck" Buckwalter at the helm. The plot of the film (which Buckwalter would say is "technically called a 'mystery film'") is almost grisly, even by modern standards.

A tramp, wandering through Cripple Creek looking for handouts, is generously welcomed into a cabin by a miner's kindly wife. She offers him food, but apparently he wants money, for he angrily strikes her down and murders her in cold blood. When the miner and his daughter return, they're grief-stricken, unable to make sense of the meaningless tragedy. The husband, vowing vengeance, forms a vigilante posse and heads out after the tramp with a pack of bloodhounds "tugging strenuously on the leash." The townspeople crest a hill, and "in the distance, Cripple Creek can plainly be seen." After a chase over bluffs, through valleys and on top of mountain ridges, and including a few major scuffles and "desperate fights," the tramp is captured. Western justice is swift. He is immediately brought to a high tree overlooking the countryside and hanged by the neck as a howling mob of miners and cowboys cheer the deed. Just to make sure there's no ambiguity as to the tramp's punishment, "[b]efore life is extinct hundreds of bullets from their revolvers pierce his body." The scene brings gasps even to modern audiences.

The extended chase through the Colorado Mountains made for a thrilling film, and it was a tremendous success. The Selig promotional material called it "the most sensational film ever made" and then, to drive home the location angle one more time, added, "The scenery is grand, making the film one of more than usual interest." Moviegoers would never accept an East Coast backdrop for a western again.

Riding high on the success of *A Lynching at Cripple Creek*, Colonel Selig was quick to put together another Colorado-themed film. The press caught the fever, too. "New subjects, new situations and new films of pictures must be constantly provided for the moving picture machines…The fast express trains, prize fights and Boer Wars having been worn threadbare, the enterprising biograph agents decided to pose a real, live thrilling Western stage coach 'hold up' in the good, old-fashioned style."

The Hold-up of the Leadville Stage ("done in 850 stirring feet of film," as Colonel Selig vividly described it) was unquestionably a western as we would know it. It had cowboys, it had a stagecoach, it had horses, it had mountain passes—it had the sort of thing that later commentators would call "the clank and jingle of spur, the banging of firearms and the rat-a-tat-tat of galloping ponies."

And it also had a newsworthy accident while filming that proved to be a promotional bonanza—so much so that, well, there were those who thought that the accident might not have been completely accidental. "Buck" Buckwalter was beginning to film the climactic moment in which bandits surround the stagecoach. The setting was Bear Creek Road, a dusty trail that had once been an actual stage route leading into Colorado Springs from the western foothills. At that moment, an actual touring car approached, occupied by a man named Mr. Aickens and his party from Philadelphia, and

The Hold-up of the Leadville Stage was arranged for the benefit of the movie camera (in the shadows at the right). Colonel Selig assembled a "picturesque company of men, women and children," while his "squad of picturesquely mounted imaginary bandits fired blank cartridges at them." *Courtesy History Colorado.*

assuming they were witnessing a genuine robbery, they began to aid in the defense of the stage passengers.

In an article headlined, "The Joke Was On the Bandits," the *San Francisco Examiner* reported on the incident: "'By gum! This is too much!' exclaimed Mr. Aickens, and blazed away at the bandits. The driver, equally indignant, let his revolver speak and the cartridges in these revolvers were not blank. Colonel Selig, who had come out of the coach with the other terror-stricken passengers, uttered a yell, and his arm dropped to his side, shot through the fleshy part. Another bullet went through a bold bandit's hat, neatly shaving his hair."

After the dust had settled a few days later, Buckwalter deadpanned, "I expect to make another picture in a day or two, and will try to send everybody in Colorado a gild-edged card of invitation, so no tenderfoots will 'butt in' at the wrong moment with a wagonload of artillery." It has since been pointed out, however, that a Mr. Aikens from Philadelphia also handled some of Colonel Selig's mail-order business through his Chicago-based merchandise house. Coincidence? You decide. In any case, the Selig Company had another hit on its hands.

The Colonel was ready to go full bore with narrative productions, but then another round of patent litigations was brought on by the Edison

A newspaper story noted that "[t]he gang that haunted that part of the old Leadville trail were just about as quick with the trigger as they make 'em." Colonel Selig directed his cast to "[g]et ready to throw up your hands and look scared!" *Courtesy History Colorado.*

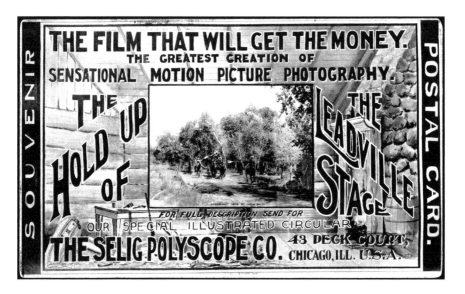

A postcard advertising *The Hold-up of the Leadville Stage* would have been mailed to movie exhibitors, tactfully suggesting that they send for "our special illustrated circular." This is how you'd market your film in the old days. *Courtesy Margaret Herrick Library, Academy of Motion Picture Arts and Sciences.*

Manufacturing Company against just about everybody in the industry. That put the brakes on narrative films for a while; Selig was gun-shy about laying out too much cash for the more costly narratives if he might just lose it again in an expensive court battle. He later mused, "During the next few years while the courts were occupied with patent litigation I confined my efforts to making scenics along different railroad lines."

As it happened, there was an international event that inadvertently brought on a new demand for those scenics and kept the Selig Company afloat for a few more years. In 1904, the world watched as St. Louis presented its World's Fair, more formally known as the Louisiana Purchase Exposition. (It was originally intended to be opened a year earlier in commemoration of the Louisiana Purchase but was postponed as the plans became larger and required an additional year to prepare.) This is the exposition that can claim to have introduced the world to the ice cream cone, peanut butter, cotton candy, Puffed Wheat cereal and Dr. Pepper.

It also introduced an eager public to what is likely the first virtual immersion ride in the world, created by George C. Hale, an engineer who had recently retired from his day job as fire chief of Kansas City. Buckwalter enthusiastically reported how the chief had "built a little amusement place on the model of a regular passenger coach with platform, interior and seats exactly like any railroad car. Then he added a rumbling motion and swing like on curves and put a motion picture sheet in front of the passengers. The sensation is the most deceptive ever seen. It is just like riding over the actual scenery." To complete the illusion, audio effects were added: steam whistles blowing, bells clanging and wheels rumbling, and electric fans would blow gusts of wind across the passengers' faces.

Hale's Tours and Scenes of the World was a runaway hit, and within a year, Hale's virtual experience "stations" were opening around the country and then around the world, until there were more than five hundred of them operating in cities from New York to Chicago, Denver, Tokyo, Mexico City, London and Paris. Anywhere from seven to nine "expeditions" were scheduled each hour, and the "cars" would usually be operating from 9:00 a.m. to 11:00 p.m.

Inside the Hale's simulator, people could "travel" to Switzerland and the Orient, and of particular delight to Buckwalter, crowds would stand in line "waiting for a chance to 'buy a ticket to Colorado' for 10 cents. Last week

All aboard for the virtual express! Hale's Tours of the World offered perhaps the first experiential amusement ride in the world. *The Moving Picture World* acknowledged, "It was difficult to realize, after such a ride, that one had not actually been in Switzerland, the illusion was so perfect. It was startling to be shunted from the luxurious Pullman out into a noisy, crowded park or busy street." *Courtesy Special Collections, University of Exeter.*

Just like attractions at theme parks today, the Hale's Tour experience began before you even entered the ride. Here, at Galveston's Electric Park, the entrance to the train-styled theater looks just like an actual railroad terminal. You can see the rear end of a "Pullman car" sticking out the back. Where in the world do you want to go? *Courtesy Rosenberg Library, Galveston, Texas.*

many of my Colorado motion pictures were shown and they made a hit, over 50,000 persons having registered through the gate."

And Colonel Selig was right on top of things. Not only was he handling the distribution of Buckwalter's films for Hale's Tours, he also had developed a specialized version of his Polyscope projector for use specifically with Hale's tour cars. It was equipped with a wide-angle lens to throw a full-sized picture from a short distance to the screen. What's more (as luck would have it), this would accommodate his specially designed translucent screen for rear projection—to complete the illusion with an out-of-sight projector (and to compensate for the often cramped space limitations of the movie ride).

Success breeds excess. Immediately, competing companies began operations with similar ideas—anything from a simulated steamboat ride to an imitation sightseeing automobile. "They have all found that Colorado views take best and my intention is to start in at once and make as many motion pictures as possible to fill the demand," Buckwalter exulted.

But we'll come back to the Hale's Tours later because there was somebody ready to amble through Colorado and into the lives of Selig and Buckwalter who would change the film industry forever. And that somebody was "Broncho Billy" Anderson. Never heard of him? Well, if you'd been a resident of just about any country in the world during the teen years of the twentieth century, you'd know exactly who he was: the biggest star in the world.

Shoot 'Em Up

Stocky, almost goofy looking, Gilbert Anderson was hardly the type you'd pick for international movie stardom. But that's exactly where he was heading when he passed through Colorado in 1907. Even at that time, he already had a pretty good pedigree of film work behind him.

Born Max Aronson of Jewish ancestry in 1880s Arkansas, he began his working life in the cotton business before heading off to New York for the glamorous world of the theater. But like so many others, the sobering reality of show business hit hard. He found little work on the stage and intermittently modeled for various artists and illustrators. His looks often had him posing for them as a cowboy, although he didn't know the first thing about riding a horse.

Following the drill, he went from agency to agency looking for work. And as most actors do when visiting an agent, he'd chirpily ask, "What's doing?" On at least one occasion, the agent replied, "There's a lot doing, but not for you." Thick-skinned, Anderson persisted. The agent asked if he'd work for fifty cents per hour. He said, "I'll work for peanuts." "Well, go down to the Edison Company; you might get a few days' work in pictures down there."

On this day, fate was on his side. He walked right into *The Great Train Robbery* itself, and you can bet that this was at the top of his résumé from that point on. The job started out inauspiciously enough. As Anderson would later remember, the director, Edwin S. Porter, asked him if he could ride. Like all overly eager actors throughout history, the city-bred Anderson exaggerated his qualifications. "Ride? I was born on a horse—and raised in a saddle."

"Well," Porter answered, "then you're one of the robbers." So, Anderson began to mount his horse in preparation for the shoot.

One of his fellow wranglers said to him, "Hey, Bud. You don't mount 'em from that side."

"What's the difference?"

"You'll find out."

Well, he hadn't gone a hundred feet before he was thrown from the horse. Incredulous, Porter said to him, "I thought you said you could ride, Anderson…You were born on a horse."

"I *was* born on a horse. Not on *this* horse."

"Well," Porter responded, perhaps a little too dryly, "you'll play different parts." And so he did, playing a total of three roles in *The Great Train Robbery*, including every actor's dream: a death scene, ruthlessly gunned down from behind by one of the brutal train robbers.

Anderson would later recall his experience at Hammerstein's Theatre on the night of one of the (many) premiere screenings in New York. It was a few blocks up the street from the theater that had hosted the premiere of Edison's Vitascope projector just seven years before. When the theater announced the picture, "people got up and started to walk to the exits. Then it started and they looked back to see what was going on, and finally they stopped. And as it progressed they started to come back to their seats and sit down. As the picture went on you could hear a pin drop…and after it was over they all, in one acclaim, gave it a rousing, rousing reception. And I said to myself: that's it; it's going to be the picture business for me."

He was as good as his word. As his aspirations expanded beyond on-camera performance and moved into actually producing and directing the movies, he became intrigued with the idea of filmmaking in general and shrewdly saw the future of motion pictures in narratives rather than the actualities and newsreels that were still so popular at the time. But it was a tough sell in the litigious atmosphere of the patent wars.

By this time, he had already changed his name from Aronson to Anderson. For years, he traveled from motion picture company to motion picture company, from New York to Pittsburgh to Chicago, sometimes being favorably received and producing his own profitable films but mostly being frustrated at the lack of cooperation—and always running into obstacles of one sort or another. That is, until he crossed paths with Colonel Selig. Selig had long seen the value of what at the time were called "story films," and he and Anderson hit it off right away, forming a prosperous working relationship.

Gilbert Anderson was willing to take on whatever role necessary to make a stage production work—even, as he himself said, going so far as being a "spear carrier." Eventually, it led him to carrying a six-shooter in his many movie cowboy roles. *Courtesy Margaret Herrick Library, Academy of Motion Picture Arts and Sciences.*

The Colonel sent Anderson to Colorado and teamed him up with the ever-dependable "Buck" Buckwalter. His horsemanship skills apparently hadn't improved much. Buckwalter noted, "When he first came here he rode a horse like a sailor—or worse." But since he was there to direct films, not star in them, this inadequacy hardly mattered.

Gilbert Anderson dug in right away and announced a slate of at least a dozen motion pictures to be filmed in the Denver region alone before moving on to other areas of the state. Denver got into the spirit of things with relish, and just like today, the movie folks attracted much attention and became favorite subjects of gushing "seen and heard" notices in the press: "During the noon hour, when the actors and 'actorines' rested for luncheon, the entire party loaded two…monster cars and came downtown to a popular restaurant. Everybody had on makeup and some wore the most lively costumes imaginable. As the two big autos rolled along the street there was much 'rubbering' and wondering what all the excitement was about."

The romantically titled *The Bandit King* was shot in Golden, just west of Denver. Anderson pressed the Overland Stage into service and had it held up for the benefit of the camera. The nearby hotel, the Overland House, was somewhat generically renamed "County Bank" and summarily robbed in the name of movie art.

Other films directed by Anderson were given equally vivid titles, such as *Western Justice* and *The Girl from Montana*, designed to pull audiences into the theaters. Despite its geographically specific title, *The Girl from Montana* was, in fact, shot in Golden, Colorado, and was intended to ride the coattails of a recent stage hit, *The Girl of the Golden West*. The take-charge heroine was played by Pansy Perry, a local society girl who, as they say, could ride a horse as well as any cowboy, and the climax of the film shows her rescuing her sweetheart from hanging by expertly shooting the rope in two just as it's pulling taut around his neck. (Take note, as this is a set piece we'll see again in later western films.)

The company was quick to publicize the economic windfall afforded by film production. The *Denver Republican* noted that "the amount of money distributed in doing this work will mean the bringing of quite a satisfactory sum of Eastern capital to this state. Some idea of this can be gained from the fact that nearly or quite $1,000 has been spent in Golden alone since the first of the year in making the pictures mentioned." Now, before we modern readers give a condescending snicker, it should be noted that in 1907, the average salary in the United States was $600 to $800 per year.

Anderson was a great showman, and he began flattering the local population right away. After the first day of shooting, he waxed poetic for the benefit of the press, perhaps a little too pretentiously. "Why, it's just like Italy with its soft light and wonderful speed for photography." As near as we can tell, Anderson had never been to Italy, but, well, that's showbiz.

Now, you may be wondering why there was this sudden burst in film production. Why were our industry stalwarts willing to tempt the wrath of Edison and face the prospect of a major lawsuit? It had to do with an industry-wide phenomenon that was fundamentally changing movie-viewing habits across the country. And it all started with two businessmen trying to find a way to turn a profit out of an unrented storefront they owned.

Harry Davis and John P. Harris were partners in both the theater and real estate businesses in Pittsburgh, Pennsylvania. In June 1905, they found themselves with a vacant storefront on their hands and were looking for a way to bring in some kind of income until they could find somebody to rent the place. Seemingly on a whim, they decided to deck it out as a theater exclusively for presenting movies. They called their improvised little theater a nickelodeon—a combination of the cost of admission (one small nickel) and the Greek word for theater (*odeon*). Clever, yes?

This was more of a radical concept than it sounds. Until this time, movies were shown as a part of vaudeville programs or at fairs or in tents set up by traveling entertainers but rarely as destination entertainment. This new theater concept would quite innocently change the face of moviegoing in America.

The film at the top of the program was *The Great Train Robbery*, still a draw two years after its initial release. The first day's business started out modestly enough, but on the second day, business tripled, and within two weeks, the partners were starting their shows at eight o'clock in the morning and running them continuously through midnight, making a profit of $1,000 per week. News spread quickly in the world of struggling entrepreneurs; all you needed was a storefront, a projector and some chairs (not mandatory), and you could start charging people to come in and look at movies. These nickel theaters began sprouting up everywhere, opening in one city and then the next until, by 1907, it was estimated that there were 2,500 to 3,000 nickelodeons in the United States. In fact, many proprietors of the Hale's Tours, which had been seeing plummeting business since their novelty wore off, began tearing out the "train car" effects mechanism and simply showing movies.

A few of the early nickelodeons left a lot to be desired in warmth and appeal. It's no wonder that some of them had the reputation for being centers of less than desirable behavior—if you get what I mean. I can't vouch one way or the other for this small storefront theater in Denver. *Courtesy Denver Public Library, Western History Department.*

The importance of the nickelodeon on the growth of the American film industry cannot be overestimated. It introduced the concept of "going to the movies" to the general population—a complete program of movies in a fixed location. Of course, theaters needed to rotate films quickly to keep audiences coming back. This increased the demand for films, and filmmakers scrambled to keep up.

Harper's Weekly commented on "the Nickel Madness" in 1907:

> *In some of the crowded quarters of the city the nickelet is cropping up almost as thickly as the saloons, and if the nickel delirium continues to maintain its hold there will be, in a few years, more of these cheap amusement-places than saloons…On one street…there are as many as five to a block…You hear in some neighborhoods of nickelodeon theater-parties. A party will set out on what might be called a moving-picture debauch, making the round of all the tawdry little show-places in the region between the hours of eight and eleven o'clock at night, at a total cost of, say thirty cents each. They will tell you afterwards that they were not bored for an instant…and after all it is an innocent amusement and a rather wholesome delirium.*

The trade magazine *The Moving Picture World* had what would prove to be a more prescient view of the situation: "They have been looked upon largely as places of trivial amusement, not calling for any serious consideration. They seem, however, to be something that may become one of the greatest forces for good or for evil in the city." Indeed, this was the moment when movies moved beyond novelty act and became a destination point in their own right, an event that marked the beginning of America's obsession with mass entertainment. It was an acceptance cycle that at least one individual in the country fully understood. Thomas Edison mused, "It has taken from seven to eight years to make room for the pictures. It takes that long to make room for the best thing ever invented. If you were to invent something tomorrow, something everybody needs, it would still take about seven years to introduce it and make room for it. I know from experience. It took me even longer to make room for the incandescent light. I guess I was about thirteen years in properly introducing the phonograph."

As more nickelodeons opened, the demand for product became even greater. More and more motion picture companies were realizing that here was a gold mine, indeed. And that's why Colonel Selig was so eager to get back into full-scale production on "story" pictures. His new producer, Gilbert Anderson, was able to crank out more than twenty films in just a little over half a year when he started working for Selig.

In our current age of inflated movie budgets, expensive special effects and lengthy contract negotiations, it's refreshing to read Anderson's account of moviemaking in the early years: "I went out, and met 'Buck' Buckwalter, and we went over to Golden, Colorado, and I figured on making a Western picture there. I got an idea and wrote a very trivial story, and looked around for somebody to play the lead. I got together a few cowboys—I had to use a couple of girls as cowboys, couldn't get enough cowboys—and I made several pictures there."

But the honeymoon was fast coming to an end for Anderson and Selig. Profits were up, but mutual trust was down. Although each would become important leaders in the ever-shifting motion picture industry over the next few years, it would not be together. There was an irreconcilable difference that would force them to go their separate ways.

You see, from his beginnings in the film business, Anderson had always wanted something bigger than what the film manufacturers were willing to offer. For years, he had worked for various film companies making contributions that would result in significant profits. What he wanted in return was more than just a regular salary and empty recognition as a valued

As the years progressed, nickelodeons became fancier and fancier. By the end of the era (the mid-1910s), some of them had designs resembling a P.T. Barnum–inspired opera house. Here, the Princess Theater towers above Curtis Street in Denver. *Courtesy Denver Public Library, Western History Department.*

employee. He wanted to own part of the company. But they were all too tightly held to give up even a tiny amount to him.

And he was now at that point with the Selig Polyscope Company. He was ready for a piece of the real pie. Of course, Colonel Selig didn't see things quite the same way, and the two parted company, on less than amicable terms. It was a rift that would last a lifetime—neither would have anything more than cursory polite words to say about the other from that point on.

Anderson headed out on his own and decided that this time, rather than trying to make his way into a company, he'd make the company himself. And he was about to embark on the unlikely partnership that would launch him into superstardom.

Pardners

George K. Spoor couldn't have known the good fortune that was ready to walk through the door of his Chicago office that spring day in 1907. He'd been involved with the film industry since its beginnings, but purely on the exhibition side of things, never as a producer. Though he no doubt appreciated the creative aspects of motion pictures, he was a businessman, and striking the deal was his forte. By 1907, he owned two businesses—the National Film Renting Company, a film exchange that rented films to exhibitors, and the Kinodrome Company, which rented projectors to vaudeville houses. His projector was in direct competition with Selig's Polyscope, and the two of them were hardly the best of friends. In fact, he had a roll of film tacked to his wall with the sprocket holes ripped completely to shreds and a sign next to it that read, "Done by the Selig Polyscope Company." Yes, there was some animosity.

But Spoor had never involved himself with the production end of motion pictures, until the rise of the nickelodeon turned the world upside down for film distributors. Spoor saw a need to change his business model. With the nickelodeon theaters booming, there was a huge clamor for more pictures. The product was becoming scarce, and Spoor was finding it increasingly difficult to turn a profit supplying films and projectors. It became very clear to him that the real money was in the hands of the people actually making the movies.

Into this situation strode Gilbert Anderson with glorious dreams of producing story pictures for the flourishing market. Spoor was intrigued with the potential profits but, ever the pragmatist, told him, "I'll put $2,500

George Spoor formed the Essanay Film Manufacturing Company with Gilbert Anderson after both had been wandering the streets of the film industry for years. Anderson later remembered, "He had a big room in the back of his office, and we put the studio there. And we started to make pictures." *Courtesy Niles Essanay Silent Film Museum.*

in it. When that's gone, you're gone." Anderson, the optimist, shot back, "That won't be gone. We'll go ahead from $2,500." They joined forces and called their company Essanay: "S" (for Spoor) and "A" (for Anderson)— get it? The partnership was, to all appearances, a somewhat uncomfortable alliance, and the two never quite seemed to trust each other fully. But the company soon began turning considerable profits, so there was little room to complain.

As it turned out, it was an extremely fortuitous time to start a new motion picture company. In that same year, negotiations were begun to settle the patent wars that had been devastating the industry for so long. In 1908, all parties involved, practically dripping with perspiration from the years of litigation, agreed to form an alliance of film manufacturers that had all previously been at war with Edison. The result was the Motion Picture Patents Company, an organization of film producers and exchanges headed by Edison himself. It was more colloquially known as "the Trust." This proved to be an enormous blessing for a company just starting out in the business. The Essanay team had seen what had happened to those who crossed the heavy hand of Edison in the past and, exercising the better part of valor, shrewdly signed into the Trust right away, avoiding the debilitating court actions that had scarred so many of the earlier filmmakers.

The Essanay Film Manufacturing Company's first film, shot in Chicago, was *An Awful Skate, or The Hobo on Rollers*, a comedy that involved a tramp (a real standard of humor in those days) trying to skate. Somewhat to Spoor's surprise, it was a huge hit. Well, that was it. Over the next few months, Anderson made a string of comedies that became the foundation of their successful production company. He filmed in Chicago until the cold, the wind and the clouds of the notorious Chicago winters kicked in.

That's when Anderson thought again of his days shooting in the sunny West. At first, he bypassed Colorado and traveled straight to California to continue shooting comedies. This was 1908, and the place that would one day be known as the movie capital of the world wasn't so hospitable to the motion picture business. He and his crew had traveled up and down the coast, and after being more or less run out of every town in which they attempted to shoot, they finally found themselves actually arrested in Los Angeles while filming a scene in which their movie comedian, attempting to catch a duck, jumps into a lake in a public park. The policeman told them, "No more taking pictures here on the streets in Los Angeles. This is a city. Go to some village and take your pictures." So it was back to Golden,

The members of the newly formed Motion Picture Patents Company gathered together for the formal signing of the deal at Thomas Edison's library in New Jersey. Edison sits triumphantly at the center. Second from the left is George Spoor, representing Essanay. Fourth from the right, just behind Edison, is Colonel Selig, bringing the Selig Polyscope Company to the table. *Courtesy Margaret Herrick Library, Academy of Motion Picture Arts and Sciences.*

Colorado. (Perhaps Anderson remembered the "Italian light.") And from that point, things began moving rather quickly.

Though Essanay was already making a name for itself with its comedies, Anderson chose to take advantage of the scenic western locale and began shooting a string of westerns, a genre that was becoming his forte. And then something happened that would turn his life around.

When he started shooting a routine western one autumn day in 1909, he didn't know just how un-routine things were going to become. The film was called *A Ranchman's Rival*. The lead actor had just received a favorable notice in the papers for his stage work and perhaps felt himself a little too important to take orders from a simple motion picture director. After Anderson insisted that he follow his directions, the actor sneered, "Why don't you pose your own pictures if you know how to do it better than I?" Anderson viewed this as an excellent suggestion and summarily fired the actor on the spot. At that point, there was nothing for him to do but take over the role himself. He was now officially producer-director-writer-star.

The plot is pretty straightforward. Our hero, a ranchman played by Gilbert Anderson, discovers that his sweetheart's affections have been co-opted by one of those modern city types—an easterner, of course. So Anderson, heartsick, decides to leave town. At the train station, he makes a most unexpected discovery: the city slicker's wife has just arrived in town, looking for her delinquent husband. Anderson races back to his sweetheart— just in the nick of time, it turns out, for he rescues her just as she's about to be married to the city boy by a bogus priest who's working in cahoots with the eastern viper.

Something about Anderson's "aw, shucks" attitude clicked with the moviegoing public, and the movie was a hit. Anderson would stay in front of the camera, eventually performing in almost four hundred cowboy pictures in his career. So, after failing as an actor on the legitimate stage, he suddenly found himself in demand on the screen. And Essanay was on its way to financial stability.

From that point on, piece by piece and movie by movie, Anderson added more bits and more set pieces and stumbled his way onto the standards that would define the movie western: the nomadic hero who drifts into the lives of the more settled populace, the moral ambiguity of the good man/ bad man hero, the endearingly awkward clumsiness displayed around the "gentler sex" and a host of other bits that characterize the genre. And how were his riding skills by this time? He himself said, "I was good enough to be thrown and break my back! I was fairly good. I never was an expert rider." From his own mouth.

But the West of the movies hadn't come unannounced. Anderson was riding the crest of a movement that, as it turns out, already had its roots deep in the American psyche. If we want to see where it came from, we don't need to look further than the other media outlets of the time to appreciate how it was poised to collide with the movie business.

How the West Won Us

G alloping across the vast plains onto the local movie screen, the western was one of the major genres stimulating the film market as the movie industry was just taking off. In 1909, *The Moving Picture World* proclaimed emphatically that "Western subjects, in which the wild and woolly plays the leading part, have won immense popularity with the people, and there has been a great and unsatisfied demand for more pictures of such a variety." And a film exhibitor declared that "all I have to do is to advertise a Western subject and I do capacity. Without them the business here would soon go to the bad." On a more personal note, after "Buck" Buckwalter took a trip to New York in 1905, he made the wry observation: "Three-fourths [of] the shows in the Broadway theaters are Western in scene and plot and they turn people away every night even at the outrageous prices they charge."

How did this happen? How did the western become a staple of moviemaking? In retrospect, it's really no wonder that the western was such a hit. Certainly since the Lewis and Clark expedition of 1803, there had been a romantic interest in the frontier and the mythos of the West. As the nineteenth century progressed, it escalated until it became practically a cultural obsession.

Anything that's that popular eventually makes its way into popular entertainment. And if we want to trace the rise of the western way back, the first noteworthy expression we find is in the dime novel of the 1800s. Dime novels (or, as they were amusingly called in Britain, penny-dreadfuls) were small books with pulpy stories centered on adventure. Subjects included frontier scouts, the American West, detectives, cowboys, Indians…you get the idea. They were cheap. As you might guess from their name, they sold for a dime—or sometimes for as little as a nickel (but later in their publication history for as much as twenty-five cents)—and appealed to a mass audience, mostly made up of males and adolescents.

Dime novels first made their appearance in the 1860s, and it wasn't long—much to the horror of people of propriety—before they soon spread into every nook and cranny of popular culture. They often featured fictional characters, but as likely as not, they would spotlight promising celebrities of the time in highly fictionalized situations. Wild Bill Hickok, Jesse James and Kit Carson made appearances in dime novels. Usually these people became even more of a celebrity simply as a result of their appearance in these pulp novels. But the one who really turned it into a gold mine—and changed the shape of entertainment in the process—was William F. "Buffalo Bill" Cody.

Buffalo Bill was a scout and buffalo hunter for the United States Army in the 1860s. Guiding a few members of European nobility and being involved in various Indian skirmishes, he made quite a name for himself with the public at large. And in a remarkable case of art imitating life imitating art, he went from celebrity to legend to icon.

The first of many dime novels featuring Buffalo Bill appeared in 1869 and proved so popular that, within four years, his exaggerated exploits had been turned into a stage play. Although many matinee idols of the day attempted to play the Indian scout on stage, there was nothing like the real thing, and at first, somewhat against his better judgment, Buffalo Bill took on the role of his lifetime: himself.

Scouts of the Prairie opened to generally withering reviews. The press acknowledged the folksy charisma of the show's star but was less impressed with the value of the production as a whole. The *Chicago Times* wrote despairingly: "On the whole, it is not probable that Chicago will ever look upon the like again. Such a combination of incongruous drama, execrable acting, renowned performers, mixed audience, intolerable stench, scalping, blood and thunder, is not likely to be vouchsafed to a city for a second time, even Chicago." But the public loved it. Or, more accurately, they loved Buffalo Bill.

Buffalo Bill played several seasons in these stage productions, known as "frontier dramas," and then in 1883, exploiting a concept that future advertising gurus would refer to as "cross-platform brand marketing," he brilliantly expanded the concept to an outdoor show called *Buffalo Bill's Wild West*, a huge extravaganza with a cast of hundreds of cowboys and Indians—incidentally setting the prototype for all Wild West shows that

It seems that every era finds something new that rots the mind of its youth. These days, we've got YouTube. A few decades back, it was comic books. But in the late nineteenth century, it was the specter of dime novels. *Courtesy Library of Congress, Prints and Photographs Division.*

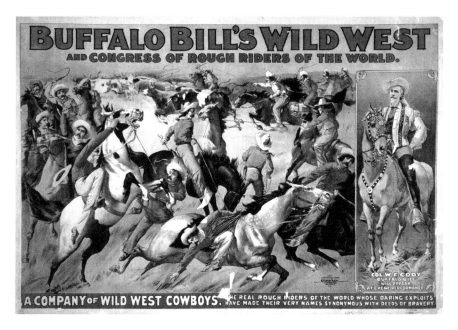

Buffalo Bill Cody packaged the West as a romantic, living spectacle for his adventure-hungry audience. *Courtesy Library of Congress, Prints and Photographs Division.*

followed. Almost single-handedly, Buffalo Bill embodied the West of the imagination that was trotting into American culture.

By the time the movies came along, the public was pretty well enamored of frontier stories that were already available in novels, theatrical productions and Wild West extravaganzas. The movies became just the latest in a string of media expressions of the public's insatiable appetite for all things western. The connection wasn't lost on film devotees of the time. *The Film Index* confidently pointed out:

> *The Essanay Company can congratulate themselves upon their enterprise in having hit upon a popular theme when they selected the West as the scene of action in their new films and the romantic cowboy to carry on the performance. A glance at the popular magazine fiction of the last few years, of any number of stage plays, which have "made good" and the quantity of these which have been eagerly devoured by the story readers and theatre-going public points out the reason why the Essanay cowboy pictures, as well as those of other manufacturers, have been so successful.*

But as audiences became more sophisticated, they also became more impatient with imitation western locales. Authenticity, or at least seeming authenticity, became a litmus test for the value of a production. This was something that couldn't convincingly be produced on the East Coast, let alone overseas, where a few film companies were attempting to cash in on the craze.

As one motion picture exhibitor of the time remarked while assessing a European release:

> *I was born in the West, have lived there for over forty years, been in every State and Territory west of the Mississippi, but never saw Indians wearing checked gingham shirts or pelts or skins for clothes, or live in huts or tents made of cornstalks, or camp in apple orchards. Neither have I seen cowboys with whiskers (they would soon be minus them, and the boys would have lots of fun doing it). Neither have I seen cowboys ride a bobtailed horse on an English saddle or carry a rifle as did the "hero" (he must have been a tenderfoot). Neither have I seen an omnibus used instead of a coach having an automobile lamp and three horses abreast….Neither will you find such beautifully paved roads in the Western States.*

It was observations like these that led to the derogatory phrase "Eastern Westerns," as well as movies that used "Jersey scenery." As Gilbert Anderson himself noted, "Some of the Eastern companies try to use the Adirondacks, but they don't get the effect that the Rockies give."

Indeed, the West proved to be a valuable commodity for filmmakers. In what would prove to be just the beginning of a trend to export American culture, within a few years, filmmakers would find themselves somewhat unwittingly exporting the West. In 1911, a commentator in *Motography* prophetically noted:

> *There is one American article of export out of which fortunes are being coined in every corner of the world, and which, under its rightful name, does not appear upon a single steamer's manifest. This is the picturesque— what is bizarre, exciting and unusual in American life, chiefly scenes of cowboys and Indians. This picturesque, a real, definite commodity of genuine commercial importance, goes with many another moving picture film across the seas, and Britisher, Frenchman, German, Spaniard, Italian, South American, Australian and South African clap their hands with joy, or*

otherwise show their approval, when the exploits of their "Yankee" brothers are flashed upon the screen…

It does not seem as if too many of these Indian and cowboy films could be fed to the moving picture goers of the rest of the world. From Liverpool to Moscow and from Stockholm to Melbourne the patrons eagerly watch the unfolding of every one of the highly colored dramas of the prairies and the mountains. It does not matter if the story is only slightly different from what they have seen before. This is the America that they have long imagined and heard about.

The crouchers on the benches of many a darkened room in far away foreign cities are quite aware that there are big cities in America teeming with gold for the worker, wonder places when one gets to them. These are not, just the same, the real America of their dreams. Outside of them, just beyond the skyscrapers, they know there is a great, open wild-land, filled with almost savage beings. Nothing like these real Americans exist anywhere else in the world. They do the maddest, most exciting things. And though the foreigner of the moving picture show does not say this in so many words, these scenes fully realize the ideal long tucked away in his head of what the Americans must be…

Europe, Asia, Africa, and all the Australias believed in the existence of the cowboy of romance, of the "Deadwood Dick," the "Alkali Ike," "Deerfoot," and "Uneas," the "big, heap, chief," the prairie wagon, the beautiful young white girl carried off by a masterful, lank savage, the squaw, the papoose, the Indian village, and, perhaps, the detachment of United States troops arriving just in time. Nothing easier. They should have them.

As a matter of fact, these exciting Western plains films do exceedingly well in this country, perhaps because of the many foreigners that crowd the moving picture theaters. They are profitable investments before they ever become articles of export. The export trade in them is fresh profit, and one that is steadily growing larger.

On Set, on Location

From 1908 through the next few years, it became a tradition for the Essanay Company to travel to Colorado to film with an itinerant company. And Gilbert Anderson was always eager to schmooze up the locals. "During the Summer we make outdoor pictures in and around Chicago, but when Fall comes, I take a photographer, property man and several principals, and follow the warm weather. Colorado is the finest place in the country for Wild West stuff."

He and his company were getting this filmmaking thing down to a regular science. After *The Ranchman's Rival*, the company made *The Heart of a Cowboy* in Morrison, Colorado, a town southwest of Denver. There were no smartphones available to snap and post any behind-the-scenes shots and stories of the day's shooting on Facebook. Fortunately, though, a Denver newspaperman who followed the troupe for a twelve-hour period gave us a firsthand account of a day in the life of a motion picture company in action in 1908. He noted with a flourish, "[F]or the benefit of those who like color and charm, interest and new sensations, a day with a 'moving picture' company is enthusiastically recommended."

The company was up bright and early to take the train from Denver to the location in Morrison, Colorado. A twenty-minute drive today was a full hour's train ride at the time. The advance crew was already at the hotel, ready to put the cast members in costume and makeup and mount them on horseback for their trek to the location down the road—a farmhouse tucked away in a copse of cottonwoods. And there, for the first time, "seated on the

What? No gaffer? No best boy? Films somehow managed to be shot with much smaller crews back in the day. Here, Gilbert Anderson directs a shoot in Morrison, Colorado, in 1909. *Courtesy Niles Essanay Silent Film Museum.*

grass," the cast would hear the plot outlined for them by Gilbert Anderson, wearing his director's hat for the moment.

The story began, appropriately, with Scene 1: "Girl comes out of house, holding some Kodak pictures of herself. Cowboy comes up, sees picture, and begs it from her. She refuses at first, but finally gives him one, writing 'To Steve' on it." And he runs through all nineteen scenes of the photoplay, all of which will be shot on that one day (so everybody had better be on their toes).

The scene descriptions could be convoluted: "Steve and Mexican quarrel over division of money. As they wrangle girl appears, learns the truth, and steps forward. Mexican starts to stab her, but she jerks revolver out of Steve's holster, and covers them both. Makes Steve hand her the money, write a confession, and then forces them to mount the same horse and jump the country." Or they could be compact: "Ride of the Vigilantes."

The main characters are referred to as "Honest Steve," "Bad Steve," "Kitty" and "the Mexican." The role of Kitty, Honest Steve's sweetheart, was played by Miss Loma Besserer, an actress from a touring stock company.

This was her first (and apparently only) experience with the "moving pictures." She began her first scene of the day demurely.

"No, no," cried Mr. Anderson. "Charming in a theater, Miss Besserer, and you certainly look a picture. But you've got to ACT a picture! This is practically pantomime, you know. Turn loose!"

"Can I talk it?" she asked.

"All you want. The machine doesn't take conversation."

And "talk it" she did. All the actors did, too. With a cavalier bravura that might make Second City Improv sit up and take note, they made up dialogue and carried on conversations as if their lines were occurring to them for the first time—in fact, that was the case. With the scene finished, they immediately moved on to the next setup, wasting no time on such unessential delays as rehearsals or retakes. And so they went through the entire morning, scene after scene, until they had nine scenes shot and it was time for lunch. Then it was back to shoot the remaining ten scenes before nightfall. (Are you a little tired just reading their schedule?) All went relatively smoothly until the cattle stealing scene.

Nowadays, a cameraman and his crew will lay down pieces of tape to mark the points of action. Out in the foothills of Colorado in 1908, the method was a little more impromptu. For the epic cattle rustling sequence, "With infinite pains Mr. Robbins placed stones and bent bushes to show the exact radius in which the cattle must be stolen, but he forgot to tell the steers. Unaware of their responsibilities and new importance, the crazy beasts bolted the picture time and again, and by the time they did get bunched, stolen and photographed, both Bad Steve and the Mexican were sorry that they had ever quit the straight and narrow path."

The pace of shooting continued relentlessly until finally, just as twilight was giving up its last light of the day, the final shot was taken. "A tired lot of players rode back to town, for every mind had been working at lightning speed, faces were weary from contortion, and all were hoarse from the rapid fire dialogue invented to help them out in their 'pantomime.' 'Oh-h-h!' sighed Miss Besserer, 'Camille is child's play to this.'"

So ended a day of shooting. And what would become of this footage from this point on? It was sent to the head office in Chicago, where it was developed, processed, edited, duplicated and leased to the motion picture houses at a set price. The first runs of the films were screened at the best picture houses in major cities, then they'd move on down to the next tier, one level lower. They'd continue "on down the line until the expiration of six months finds them delighting the Podunk populace." At the end of six

The Essanay cast and crew on location. Gilbert Anderson proudly declared, "We are well equipped, or soon will be, for making some of the best Western subjects ever released by any company…Good scene painters are on the job, and people who can act, cowboys who can ride, women who can shoot, have been employed." What more could a film crew want? *Courtesy Niles Essanay Silent Film Museum.*

months, the films were pretty much worn out and would be returned to Chicago to be "melted up," a procedure used to recover the silver used in the image rendering process. Essanay would net about $2,000 per year from this recovery process. This gives us a hint of just one more reason why so many of these early films are lost to us. A sound business decision at the time resulted in the unfortunate loss of a large piece of our cultural heritage.

With its prospects looking great, Essanay upped its production schedule and now had two units shooting simultaneously: the western unit produced more westerns, while a Chicago unit produced urban dramas and comedies. They were released at the rate of two per week, the westerns issued on Saturdays and the comedies issued on Wednesdays.

But the film world is a small place. And just over the horizon, Anderson's fiercest competitor was about to return to Colorado.

Under the Stars

While Gilbert Anderson and his Essanay Company were blazing a trail to prosperity, Colonel Selig wasn't just sitting on his hands back in Chicago. His Polyscope Company was also a signatory to the Motion Picture Patents deal and was finally free from the money-draining revolving door of litigation. He immediately embarked on a full-scale production schedule. He'd built a new studio in Chicago, and although he kept things busy there—certainly trying to amortize the costs—he didn't waste much time in sending a unit to his much-treasured Colorado locations. Buckwalter was still there, still extolling the virtues of his adopted home: "The State has pictorial wonders that have scarcely been seen. In Colorado it is not a lack of subjects but a case of selection."

There was perhaps an unstated competition between Selig and Anderson as they both rode to fame and fortune following the western trail. Their two companies became the gold standard for westerns, and *The Moving Picture World* noted that the paper's office boy had one single-minded ambition: "[S]ome day he hopes to ride a bucking broncho and take part in some of the Wild West productions of Selig and Essanay, which he never misses seeing and says are 'the whole cheese.'" High praise, indeed.

Colonel Selig now had a regular troupe of actors that he would send off to take part in his location westerns. He'd usually augment this ensemble with actors from the local stock companies or touring theater performers. It's true that motion pictures were still considered bottom-of-the-barrel work to the thespians of the legitimate stage, but not the paychecks. Buckwalter observed, "A year ago I made ten pictures...and had practically the entire bunch of actors from the Brandon Theatre working in the scenes. And the amusing part of this was that the actors had not seen real money for six or seven weeks before I began on the pictures. A trick bicycle rider from the Orpheum got more for ten minutes' work than he got for a whole week on the circuit."

And to really add authenticity to a western, there was nothing like the inclusion of "off duty" professional cowboys and rodeo performers. The pay was better than what they could make on the ranch, and the work became so steady that "[d]emand for cowboys, in moving pictures, is driving Western ranchers into raising wheat, instead of cattle. The spectacle of a ranchman paying ten cents to see cowboys killing valuable time, doing stunts and making love, shows how great has been the fall of the mighty." In time, Selig even went so far as to hire the entire cast of a Wild West show—one of the many that were inspired by Buffalo Bill's original spectacular.

In 1910, Selig struck platinum when he hired a relatively unknown and aimless drifter to wrangle the horses for one of his productions. This rootless cowboy had been wandering from ranch to rodeo to Wild West show for years. He was someone who would ultimately push Gilbert Anderson out of the national consciousness as America's definitive cowboy. And his name was Tom Mix. He brought the kind of costumes and stunt action used in live Wild West shows to Selig film productions and would become the top cowboy star over the next two decades.

Tom Mix led two lives. There was the official studio publicity life that would be expanded and added onto as Tom advanced his career—a fabulous tale of adventure and heroics. And then there was the actual life, far from ordinary but much less spectacular. Let's take a look at each in their turn, since they share the lead character, though little else.

The official life was indeed a wonder—something that every living, breathing American male would have liked to claim for his own. Ready? Here's the "authorized" life of Tom Mix. According to this version, his father was Captain Mix, "of the hellroaring Seventh United States Cavalry, a veteran wounded at the battle of Wounded Knee." With such noble parentage, Tom attended the Virginia Military Institute and then became a member of Teddy Roosevelt's Rough Riders and "went to Cuba as a scout in the Spanish-American war, thence to the Philippines and on to the fighting in China at the battle of Tien-Tsin." Heading back to the States, Tom found himself bored by civilian life, so he turned his gaze to the West and joined the Texas Rangers, with whom he was wounded multiple times in gunfights with bandits and rustlers. And somewhere in the middle of all this, he found

Tom Mix approached everything he did with enthusiasm and swagger. He was definitely his own man, and midway through his career, he said, "I've been Tom Mix all my life and I'll be Tom Mix for the rest of it." *Courtesy Library of Congress, Prints and Photographs Division.*

time to become a part of the Boer War and then the Mexican Revolution as a part of Madero's Rebels (or possibly with Pancho Villa himself). Oh yes, he was also sheriff of multiple counties and jurisdictions.

Now, even when we try to piece together something that would pass as the real version, the best we can hope for is what we might call the likely version. Trying to track down the actual man leads us on a road of obscure references and partial documentation so that by the time we're ready to draw some conclusion as to what it is we can really be sure of, the answer comes back as "not much." There are certain things that are well documented and others that are, well, just well interpreted. Even researching actual records reveals conflicting stories.

Ready? The "true" story goes more or less like this. His father was the stable master for a wealthy lumber baron, and from an early age, Tom became quite familiar with horses and equestrian skills. (So, unlike Gilbert Anderson, he actually was practically born on a horse.) He did serve in the military, but not quite to the extent that his official story would like us to believe. In 1898, as things started heating up leading into the Spanish-American War, he enlisted in the U.S. Artillery, although he never saw action. His unit never went overseas. In 1902, he took an extended furlough to marry his second wife and never returned. He was listed as AWOL and then as a full-blown deserter, and it's a bit of a mystery why the army never pressed charges. He worked at various odd jobs in Oklahoma—bartending, some sheriff work and a few stints as a ranch hand. He was particularly proficient at riding and roping, placing first in numerous rodeo competitions in Arizona, Colorado and Oklahoma. Because of these skills, he worked quite a bit with the numerous Wild West shows that were still a common form of entertainment at the time.

It's here where his two lives converge. While working as a performer for the Circle D Ranch Wild West Show, he was hired by the Selig Polyscope Company to wrangle the animals for a film it was shooting, and he took to the motion picture world like butter melting into warm cornbread.

There's one thing we can be certain of with Tom Mix: he was not shy. Even though he started out as the animal wrangler for the film crew, it wasn't long before he had boisterously worked his way to the front of the camera. He watched the production from behind the scenes for a while and then approached Francis Boggs, Selig's director. As he told it, "[W]hen some fancy-looking dude from the East, who was playing hero, decided that he couldn't take any risks with his precious face, I pushed myself forward in my usual modest way, and whispered, 'Say, boss, I'll do them horse-jumps for you!' And that was the way I broke into movies!"

Tom Mix was everything Gilbert Anderson wasn't—brash, rugged, athletic and swaggering. While Anderson did his best to *act* the part of cowboy, Tom Mix *was* a cowboy. Anderson, perhaps a bit jealous, had his own opinion: "An excellent rider but a bad actor." Perhaps so. But no matter what your estimation may have been as to his acting skills (and opinions tended to run to the negative), he was a dynamo on the screen. In that first film, he "roped and bulldogged a steer in a close-up in the matter of sixteen seconds."

Tom Mix had no aspirations beyond performing. He had no desire to direct, write or own part of the company. This was something that sat very well with Colonel Selig. He now had a recognizable star who would draw the crowds to his films and increase their profitability, and the Colonel was happy to give him just about anything he wanted—just so long as it didn't involve any control of the business.

If Tom Mix's official biography sounds a bit beyond belief, we have to remember that this was the age of ballyhoo. With publicity machines running unchecked by social media or TMZ and no ethical concerns whatsoever, filmmakers would create life stories for their stars that were as fanciful as the movies in which they played. The stars themselves became characters for the sake of their fans.

This was about the time that film companies were realizing the box office power of their stars. The live theater had long relied on big-name celebrities to attract an audience and sell tickets, even going so far as to hire celebrities from other fields to appear on the stage (as was the case with Buffalo Bill). The very early movies had little occasion to use such a practice, as their content tended to be more event driven (as in the ubiquitous "fire run") or plot driven (as in narrative stories such as *Tracked by Bloodhounds*). Occasionally, the actualities and "newsreels" of the day would include footage of presidents or diplomats.

But as we get to the end of that first decade of the twentieth century, the public began to become aware of the actors. In 1909, *The Moving Picture World* observed:

> *Up-to-date moving picture places have adopted the ancient custom of regular play houses in placing in the lobbies of the theater large frames containing photographs of the leading people in various film subjects...The patrons of the picture houses have at last become convinced that the pictures are made from posing by regular actors and actresses and that they are reproductions of regular performers. This has led to the bringing forward of personal identity of the people engaged in the production.*

In fact, not unlike today, fans could become, well, fanatic:

> *I am told by a manufacturer that many letters are received from men asking the names and addresses of women taking parts in the pictures and they do not shield the purpose for which the information is asked. At the same time it's stated that the inquiries are very respectfully made and the writers' evince a strong disposition to pop the question...One manufacturer showed me a letter written by a farmer in a Western State. He asked the manufacturer to intercede for him and facilitate the opening of correspondence. He said he had watched his favorite in the pictures for weeks and every new picture increased the fascination. As evidence of good faith, he offered to sell his farm, travel East and open a picture house convenient to the abiding place of the actress whose acquaintance he sought. "It beats the Dutch," the*

Gilbert Anderson, businessman. As part owner of the Essanay Film Manufacturing Company, Anderson adopted the demeanor of urbane entrepreneur. *Courtesy Margaret Herrick Library, Academy of Motion Picture Arts and Sciences.*

Gilbert "Broncho Billy" Anderson, motion picture cowboy. As movie star, the *San Francisco Chronicle* declared him to be "[t]he king of the movies, whose position in the film industry is unsurpassed and whose face is seen oftener in the world than that of any other American." Wow. *Courtesy Margaret Herrick Library, Academy of Motion Picture Arts and Sciences.*

manufacturer said. "Why, the lady he wants to meet is happily married and is the mother of four children."

George Spoor got a hint of the power of screen personality when he and Gilbert Anderson were chatting outside a hotel one day. A stranger approached Anderson and began, "Are you—?" Without waiting for him to finish, Anderson completed the sentence. "Yes, I am the man in the pictures." George Spoor related this incident to a reporter while in London on his way to Paris and then Berlin to oversee operations of the Essanay distribution market. And the fact that he brought it up indicates how well known the Gilbert Anderson cowboy character was becoming throughout the world.

It was about this time that Gilbert Anderson created the character of "Broncho Billy" Anderson—played, of course, by himself. The character made its debut in *Broncho Billy's Redemption*, released in July 1910. By his own admission, Anderson somewhat plagiarized the character from a *Saturday Evening Post* story. While reading the article, he took note of the particular story structure, and inspiration struck him to "get a central character and build your story around him." And that's exactly what he did.

Broncho Billy was, as Gilbert Anderson called him, "a sort of a Robin Hood outlaw," and rather quickly, the star turned into the character in the public's eye. It was this character, more so than Gilbert Anderson himself, who became the international celebrity. Before the series was finished, Anderson would create almost four hundred two-reel episodes. "It went like wildfire. They couldn't get enough of them…I centralized the character, somebody they could heroize and love."

As it turns out, the timing was perfect.

The Movie Machine

In 1908, "Buck" Buckwalter observed, "The picture show business has developed into a most astonishing industry throughout the country. Everywhere it is flourishing. It is the poor man's grand opera." Or, as *The Moving Picture World* more pragmatically put it:

> *Rapid growth of an industrial enterprise scarcely attracts attention here in America. We have come to look upon rapidity of development as an inherent right, and so it is…The vogue of motion pictures, the poor man's natural amusement and privilege, has probably grown more rapidly than any other one field of endeavor one could call to mind, and still the giant stride it has made was the natural outcome of supply and demand and therefore a natural and not a forced development.*

Motion pictures were becoming the national pastime. And what kind of movies were people flocking to see? It seems the western films of Selig and Anderson had lit a fire under the moviegoing public, so much so that every film company was looking to inject a little western color into their films. The West became fully crowded with film crews, shooting from Oklahoma to Arizona to Colorado—looking for the perfect sunset, mountain, plains and sagebrush to put behind their actors. There were so many of them filming in the same locations it's a wonder they didn't trip over one another.

In 1909, in response to the growing demand of the nickelodeon theaters, Selig ferociously increased film production to the rate of two new films a week. Within months, Anderson and Spoor's Essanay Company was doing

No one today knows who these people were or what they were filming. But it's a timeless evocation of the draw that the expansive West had on the imagination of early filmmakers. As director Cecil B. DeMille would later describe it, "Imagine, the horizon is your stage limit and the sky your gridiron. No height limit, no close-fitting exits, no conserving of stage space, just the whole world open to you as a stage." *Courtesy History Colorado.*

the same. The race was on. In 1911, Essanay raised its output to three films a week. Selig countered with four releases and then, in December 1912, announced that he'd be releasing an astonishing five pictures each week.

It wasn't just audience demand that was fueling the growth in location shooting in the West; it was also production expediency. This was years before indoor studio lighting would become practical, so filmmakers needed sunlight to shoot and plenty of it. In order to get as much sunlight as they could for their interior scenes, they constructed large, glass-encased studios that looked more like greenhouses than film factories. But not every scene of every movie could be an interior. And exterior shooting in Chicago or New York, as we've seen, could sometimes be a hit-and-miss affair, owing to the often-hazy atmosphere and inclement winters. So, no matter how many

Movie companies would run ads for their films in the trade papers. Here, Selig lists his slate of films for the week of December 17, 1912, including a squib for *Buck's Romance*, a "virile western story with a strong comedy side to it." *Courtesy Norlin Library, University of Colorado.*

scripts they may have had in the hopper ready to shoot, they could not keep a regular shooting schedule due to the weather.

The rise in popularity of the western, then, was quite fortuitous for the filmmakers. It gave them a subject that could logically be shot in locations with more continuous sunlight. And that brought moviemakers to the sunny West. (You remember Buckwalter's trolley shot during a Denver winter.) Now, what sort of films would a filmmaker likely shoot in the West? Taking advantage of the props and sets at hand, westerns were the perfect match. Pretty soon the whole thing was rolling along with the alacrity of a spinning tumbleweed.

These early westerns had a freewheeling sense of humor that grew directly from their frontier origins. Their gloriously absurd plots never made any pretense of being anything other than what they were. In *Buck's Romance*, a Selig western from 1912, the hero wins an Indian princess as payment for a gambling debt, despite the fact that he's already married. Filled with the self-assured attitudes of the times, the film is still an engagingly lighthearted look at a world only a few decades removed from our own. The cast was made up of performers who would later become

An intriguing still from *Buck's Romance*. That's Myrtle Stedman sitting at William Duncan's feet. Stedman became a minor Hollywood silent beauty, although she would occasionally return to the light opera stage. Duncan also followed the movies to Hollywood and became a well-paid leading man in the late teens and early 1920s but eventually went on to character parts, mostly in westerns. *Courtesy Margaret Herrick Library, Academy of Motion Picture Arts and Sciences.*

regular Hollywood character actors, including William Duncan and Myrtle Stedman. And, of course, the role of Buck's horse was played by "Kid."

The film *A Matrimonial Deluge* has a plot reminiscent of Shakespeare: our hero, jilted by his sweetheart, advertises for a bride, and the response is phenomenal. But the original sweetheart shows up in disguise and wins back the heart of our hero. All's well that ends well, as all the cowboys of the valley and all the would-be brides match up for a true "matrimonial deluge."

The Film Index proclaimed, "Since last Fall, when the Essanay Company established a branch producing staff right out in the plains and foothills of the West the unceasing cry of the exhibitor was 'Bully, keep it up! It's just what we want!' And, although several other manufacturers entered the field there was no murmur nor hint that the cowboy picture was being overdone."

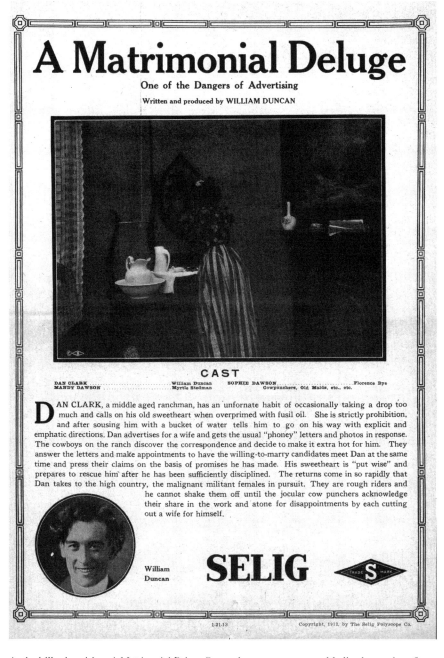

A playbill advertising *A Matrimonial Deluge*. Some theater owners would clip the stories of the films from the pages of *The Moving Picture World* and exhibit them on bulletin boards in front of their theaters. But by the early 1910s, film manufacturers were printing posters for exhibitors to promote forthcoming movies. *Courtesy Margaret Herrick Library, Academy of Motion Picture Arts and Sciences.*

This astonishing acceleration of output began to take its toll on production resources. By 1910, it was standard practice for filmmakers to shoot their films piecemeal at various locations across the country. Usually, the company would shoot the interiors at its home base using its glass studios. Then it would travel to various locations around the West to shoot exteriors. It would stay a few weeks or months and then move on, depending on the weather (or the reception of the local populace). And in those days before digital filming, when a negative was shot in the field, it had to be sent back to the main office to be developed. It was a cumbersome system—shooting interiors in the studio at one time of the year and shooting exteriors at another time when the company was on the road, as well as having the additional burden of sending the film back to the home base to be developed. Film production became a long, strung-out procedure. It could take months to get one simple film into the theaters no matter how quickly and efficiently each of the individual steps was handled.

That's why in 1910, Gilbert Anderson came up with a nifty little innovation that would set Essanay apart from any other filmmaking

The Essanay cowboy cast prepares itself for a shoot on location in the Rockies. Behind them is their brand-spanking-new portable stage for shooting interiors out-of-doors. If you look closely, you can see a scrim stretched over the top to diffuse the harsh sunlight. *Courtesy Niles Essanay Silent Film Museum.*

Here's the portable stage in action, shooting a scene from *Circle C Ranch's Wedding Present* in 1910. Note how they're still making use of a somewhat fake-looking painted backdrop. The film is intended to be a light comic western, but still, moviemakers wouldn't be able to get away with such onscreen artificiality for much longer. *Courtesy Niles Essanay Silent Film Museum.*

operations traveling the country at the time. Competition then was as fierce as it is today, and any little trick could make a difference. Anderson had been shooting at various western locations including Montana, Wyoming, Oregon, California and Mexico. He came back to Colorado and declared that he "had some big stuff in mind and needed a little Colorado local color." He brought with him not only his company of twenty-five people but also a technological ace up his sleeve: a self-contained, portable production facility "conveyed in a specially constructed Essanay 60 foot baggage car, in which can be stowed 12,000 lbs. of baggage."

This car had everything a location unit could wish for. It had a portable stage that could be assembled in any location for shooting interiors on the spot. This stage was specially designed to fold up—framework, walls, canvas roof and all—into a precise space easy for shipping in the specially built baggage car. It had the props and equipment necessary for shooting exteriors wherever the train found itself. It had a laboratory for developing

Mutt and Jeff were popular comic strip characters in the early twentieth century. Essanay answered with its own movie take on the theme with the Hank and Lank series, most of which were shot at the Essanay Chicago studio. The comedies were somewhat urban in nature and this one, *Sandwich Men*, was the only one shot in Colorado. *Courtesy Niles Essanay Silent Film Museum.*

negatives on the spot. It had a cutting room to edit films. In the bottom-line terms of efficient film production, this outlay set the Essanay team way ahead of its competitors. All of its productions could now be handled in one continuous flow from start to finish. No longer was it necessary to shoot interiors in Chicago and then shoot the exteriors a few months down the line and go through the mess of shipping the unprocessed negatives back to the Chicago offices for development. It speeded up the production process immeasurably.

Anderson meant business. He boasted that he would "break all records in the line of Western pictures." He'd go chugging through Colorado and other western states on his rolling all-in-one studio, releasing his westerns far more efficiently and inexpensively than his rivals could even dream of. He proclaimed to the world that "Colorado is the finest place in the country for Wild West stuff."

And yet, in just a short time, he'd be leaving Colorado for good, as would Colonel Selig and most of the other filmmakers. This little business decision would change the motion picture outlook in Colorado—and the nation—for all time.

The Movies Went Thataway

It seems to be a particular trait in all of us that, when looking at events of the past, we tend to infuse some sense of the inevitable in the results, as if everything was heading in that direction from the start. And so it seems with the early American film industry. We see the various pioneering filmmakers haphazardly moving across the West, crisscrossing their own paths, generally heading toward the Pacific, and we think, "Ah, they were looking for Hollywood. What took them so long to get there?" And though in a sort of figurative sense, they probably *were* looking for the metaphorical concept of Hollywood, what they were mostly doing was just wandering.

Both Selig Polyscope and Essanay undoubtedly viewed themselves as being based squarely in Chicago. That's where they had their main studios, and that's where they shot most of their interiors. The traveling troupes were simply that. They would journey throughout Colorado and the West searching for good backgrounds in which to shoot and then return to their home base of Chicago to regroup, debrief and prepare for their next set of films. They weren't traveling across the West looking for a place to land, and they certainly weren't looking for a place to set up a studio. They already had one of those. But eventually Hollywood found *them*, and the film industry found a new home.

As early as December 1907, Colonel Selig had shot one tiny scene for his epic, *Monte Cristo* (based on a stage version of *The Count of Monte Cristo*), in the waters off the California coastline. The rest of the film had been shot largely on interior, painted sets back in Chicago, and this scene was inserted, somewhat jarringly, into the middle of it. Film historians like to point to this as the very first narrative film shot in "Hollywood," although to be fair, in the mind of the filmmaker himself, this shoot was just one of many locations he'd used across the country, and it's only in hindsight that it takes on historic importance.

More significantly, it was a year and a half later, in March 1909, that one of Selig's film units went to Los Angeles and set up a provisional shop in the back of a Chinese laundry. Apparently, something was in the works because soon thereafter, Selig bought some land nearby and began building a permanent studio as an adjunct to his Chicago facilities. On August 24, 1909 (a truly historic date), the western branch of the Selig Polyscope Company moved into its new, though still incomplete, facilities in Hollywood, California (actually, technically, a little east of there in a Los Angeles neighborhood now known as Silverlake). "Just a crossroads out in the country" is how film pioneer Mack Sennett would later describe the Hollywood of the time.

The Colonel later recalled the significance of his move to California. "After we tried our luck in the West, others weren't long in following suit." History would prove how right he was.

The choice of California simply made economic sense to the Colonel—a back lot ready-made with oceans, mountains, plains and cities. But the movie business was in a tremendous flux, and nobody could really be certain what direction the industry would take. For all anybody knew, film companies were ready to set up ancillary branches all throughout the country. So, even with two complete facilities humming at full speed, Colonel Selig continued shooting in Colorado and teasingly held out the possibility of actually opening a studio there.

The Selig Colorado production unit was based in Cañon City, in the south-central part of the state. By 1911, they were becoming a part of the community, invited to social events, teas, dinners and the like. The Selig Company returned the favor by doing what it did best: entertain. It performed at charity events and took part in various public demonstrations for the amusement of the citizens. Tom Mix figured heavily in the consciousness of the people. In one outdoor event, "Mr. Mix was driven in an automobile at a high rate of speed to within a few feet of the steer selected for the experiment when he leaped from the machine to the back of the animal and threw it to the ground…The whole thing was done so quickly as to astonish spectators." I'd have been astonished too.

And often, so the story goes, Tom and his fellow actors would cut loose at the local saloon. Nowadays, the kinds of games you find in bars consist of foosball or darts or pinball. In those days, though, and in that location, the great amusement was to place lemons in shot glasses lined up at the end of the bar and try to best one another at shooting the lemons out of the glasses. The loser bought drinks for everyone.

There were constant hints from the company that building a studio in this land of mild climate and bright sun was imminent and that "nowhere in the United States are the surroundings more adaptable for securing a wide range of pictures than here and that fact, coupled with the unusual number of bright cloudless days, renders Cañon City an almost ideal place for the successful prosecution of the company's business." A large building would be needed to house the company, and scores of people would be hired to help process the film.

So it probably came as a surprise to the Cañon City community in January 1913 when Selig picked up his production unit, Tom Mix and all, and left Colorado with a vague sort of promise that he'd return. He never did.

Broncho Billy Anderson had also been flirting with the suitability of California for shooting moving pictures. After his successful use of the production car in Colorado, he left the state in October 1910 to do a little

A Selig promotional train chugs westward, and with it, at least symbolically, the movie dream travels to Hollywood. *Courtesy History Colorado.*

shooting around other parts of the West. He found himself in California and flitted from one shooting location to another over a period of years—a few months in Los Gatos, then a few months in Redlands and a while in Santa Monica, San Rafael and Lakeside. It was all becoming so nomadic that the company probably breathed a sigh of relief in 1912 when the production unit finally settled for good in Niles, California, a few miles southwest of San Francisco. Here, Essanay set up its permanent western headquarters. Colorado had been lost in the shuffle; Anderson would never return there to shoot.

One by one, locations around the country were succumbing to Hollywood centralization. Within a few years, even Chicago would give way. With movie production following more of a linear structure, the players needed all the elements with them at hand. Anderson's mobile lab had made this clear. Smaller cities and towns across the country just couldn't keep up, boosterism to the contrary. Colorado, like other sites throughout the West, had never really been a production hub per se but was rather what we might call a very, very distant shooting location.

But Colorado wasn't about to be left on the cutting room floor. Some of the alumni from Selig's western unit stayed behind to patch a new film company together. One of them in particular would be instrumental in keeping Colorado on the silver screen for at least a few more years.

Can-Do Attitude

Otis B. Thayer became a film producer by accident. Like so many before him, he had wandered into film production through the back door as an actor. By the time he entered movies, he'd already seen decades on the live stage in melodramas and musicals, touring the theater circuits in such syrupy chestnuts as *Sweet Clover*, a musical of minor proportions but a steady income for him. No one knows exactly how he first drifted into movies, but with almost twenty years' seniority on both Tom Mix and Gilbert Anderson, Thayer wasn't exactly in a position to be playing juveniles. So, by 1911, he had been hired by the Selig Company to fill the "character" parts in its productions. In September that year, Colonel Selig sent a company of twenty professionals—actors, actresses, camera operators, scenic artists and others—on a shooting expedition throughout Wyoming and Colorado. Early on, the company's resident director left the group, and Otis Thayer took over those duties. Having been on the stage most of his life, he'd probably seen it all, and he stepped into his new role with ease.

When Selig decided to move his western unit on to California, Thayer stayed in Colorado and joined a number of Colorado entrepreneurs who had made up their minds to get in on some of the lucrative movie action themselves. They started their own film enterprise and called it the Cheyenne Motion Picture Company. Now, this is a noteworthy development. Unlike the Selig Company or Essanay, which were based in Chicago, the Cheyenne Motion Picture Company was actually headquartered in the West, where shooting was taking place.

Otis B. Thayer, known informally as "Obie," works with his cowboy players. The ranchmen are inspecting some precious stones that will figure into the plot of the movie. *Courtesy Denver Public Library, Western History Department.*

The folks of little Cañon City couldn't have been more excited. The August 8, 1912 *Cañon City Record* gushed:

> *The Cheyenne people intend to make their own pictures in every particular and the location of the studio here would bring at least twenty-five motion picture actors and actresses to the city, not counting the men connected with the mechanical department.*
>
> *Mr. Thayer stated that it would be a big enterprise for the town for the pay roll would amount to about ten thousand dollars each month. It would give employment to a good many Canon City people and would be a great help in every way...*
>
> *Mr. Carroll and Mr. Thayer are both boosting for Canon for all they are worth and the business men of this city are giving them every encouragement possible. If the plant is to be located here, the matter will be decided within the next four months and construction will commence soon afterwards.*

Although he was now a full-fledged movie producer, Obie Thayer, like so many film people, still wore multiple hats. Here, at right, he's assuming an on-camera role for a Colorado Motion Picture Company film. Josephine West looks determinedly thoughtful. *Courtesy Denver Public Library, Western History Department.*

As events transpired, the bulk of the company's shooting schedule took place in Wyoming. But in any case, after two releases, the company went out of business. Such is the nature of entrepreneurial ventures. This wasn't unusual for the times; somewhat like today's startup mobile app and web design companies, motion pictures were the hot new thing to do, and film companies were coming and going, restructuring and reorganizing and reforming on a regular basis. In those entrepreneurial times, just like our own times, a number of film companies sprouted into existence only to close their doors within months.

There followed a blur of film companies with names such as the Pikes Peak Film Company and the Columbine Film Company all shooting up and down the Front Range of the Rocky Mountains. And Otis Thayer, ever the scrappy entrepreneur, was involved with each of them.

Interestingly, some of the films produced at this time dealt with urban social issues, not a normal subject for a Colorado film but one that reflected the trend of movies at the time to present morality tales of social relevance.

Saved by the Juvenile Court starred an actual judge, Judge Ben Lindsey, a controversial social reformer who advocated for fairness in juvenile issues and family justice.

The plot, synopsized by the distribution company, presents two parallel stories, one showing the "bad" way to handle juvenile offenders in the courts and the other showing the "good" way. In the first story, a fourteen-year-old petty offender is brought before the court and, strictly according to the law, is sentenced to six months in jail, where, by association, he becomes a hardened criminal. When he's released, he commits a more heinous crime and is shot, "thus ending a life that might have had a successful career."

In the second story, a young boy and his sister are brought before reform judge Lindsey, who instead sends them each to specialized schools, where they are "trained along instructive lines." Once they're reintroduced back into society, they find more conventional lines of work and ultimately meet their own special sweethearts. In the end, "Judge Lindsey is called upon to officiate at a double wedding." Thus ended Colorado's foray into urban drama, and although the film enjoyed a reasonable success, thus ended another local film company.

Obie Thayer lines up a shot, circa 1912—a nice glimpse into a small studio setup of the times, showing multiple sets assembled and ready to go. The scenery betrays its lineage from stage sets but will have a reasonably solid look when filmed. *Courtesy Denver Public Library, Western History Department.*

Each film company, in turn, would fall to the wayside. But the one that would really have a game-changing effect on the motion picture industry in the Rockies was the Colorado Motion Picture Company—headed, of course, by Otis Thayer. The Colorado Motion Picture Company began operations in 1913 with a contract from the Warner brothers (yes, *those* Warner brothers) to produce one feature film every three weeks for their then fledgling film distribution business.

Things started off on a positive note for the company, but that would soon change. Their first film was a hit called *Pirates of the Plains*, a movie that any film company at the time could have been proud of. True, the plot was just a bit rusty: two brothers, one good, one bad; one is blamed for the crime of the other. In the end, a pistol-packing sweetheart saves him from hanging in the nick of time. Sound familiar? We've seen variations of this plot wend their way throughout the history of the movies. But *Pirates of the Plains* added a few inventive nuances of its own, employing relatively sophisticated crosscutting techniques to build suspense in its adventure-filled story and fully utilizing the talents of its young heroine, Josephine West.

The Colorado Motion Picture Company confidently set up shop in Cañon City in 1913. That's Otis Thayer, the indefatigable ringleader of the organization, on the car's running board to the right. *Courtesy Denver Public Library, Western History Department.*

Incidentally, there was a reason that films like this developed women as strong central characters. Movie theaters and other public places were still fighting the reputation of being slightly shady establishments where women had better watch their step. The movies encouraged the patronage of women by incorporating them as lead characters. In many films, including *Pirates of the Plains*, women not only have strong roles but also often take the initiative in resolving the plot.

The film was a hit, and the future looked promising indeed. But very quickly, things took a severe turn for the worse with an on-location accident that would cast a pall over Colorado filmmaking and regional filmmaking in general for years to come.

Danger and the threat of injury were facts of life for these early filmmakers. Broncho Billy Anderson acknowledged as much when he told *The Moving Picture World*, "In desperate riding and driving it is a wonder that someone is not injured in every picture we take." Still, there was enough danger to go around. Injuries were being reported in the press on a disarmingly regular basis. Insurance companies wouldn't even issue policies to actors due to the high risks involved in their day-to-day activities.

A classic pose from a Colorado film. That's Josephine West holding the hanging party at bay. Unlike many of her peers, she chose not to continue in motion pictures, and after a number of starring roles in Colorado films, she more or less disappeared from the movie world. *Courtesy Denver Public Library, Western History Department.*

Commutes come in all shapes and sizes, but here we see one of the more unusual approaches used to travel to a movie location in Colorado. Beats taking a bus. *Courtesy Denver Public Library, Western History Department.*

Even a short list can be somewhat disconcerting. In December 1912, the Selig Company was filming a stagecoach navigating a hilly incline near a river. The coach had sixteen cast members aboard, and perhaps the distribution was a little off—four riding inside and twelve perched on top. Yes, it might have been a little top-heavy. As it crested a steep embankment, it began to sway and tip, hurtling all passengers down the rocky precipice.

Even Rex DeRosselli, a seasoned veteran of filmmaking, was shaken as he watched the incident from a nearby hill:

> I have been in the motion picture business a long time and have seen so many accidents that I am somewhat hardened to them and rarely am afraid, but yesterday when I saw the stage tipping I believe my heart actually stood still…The possibilities of a bad accident were so great that I found myself covering my eyes as the coach tipped. However, the coach tipped slowly and enabled many to jump. That is all that saved them. A box of red apples on the top of the coach broke open and were scattered down the incline. To me they looked like rivulets of blood trickling down a battle-stormed parapet.

Everybody laughed after they picked themselves up because then they saw the funny side.

They didn't laugh so hard over the next few days as their bruises and sprains began to set and swell. The good news, though, was that the cameraman, evidently transfixed by the mesmerizing events before him, kept cranking his camera and, as the press reported, "produced a fine picture of the thrilling scene."

Shortly thereafter, William Duncan, a leading man of several Selig westerns and party to the tipping coach incident, had his horse fall on him while filming a chase for the camera. Several ligaments in his arm were torn; he was rendered unconscious and taken to the hospital. The paper noted that this was his third accident within the last month as, "about three weeks ago, he was accidentally shot while engaged in producing a Cam-drama."

Joe Ryan, another leading man, was involved in what the local press referred to as his "hoo doo" picture, for, "at least twice he was trampled by the horse of the leading lady and one time he was forced to stay in the hospital four or five days because while riding fiercely at the head of a band of cowboys his horse stepped in a gopher hole precipitating him to the ground, and before the other cowboys could draw up he was trampled into unconsciousness by their horses. He received enough injuries in this picture to kill an ordinary man."

Ben Turpin, a comedian of the silent cinema, perhaps summed up the movie business attitude best when he said, "This is a great life. I have been in the moving picture biz working for Essanay for two years, and I must say I had many a good fall, and many a good bump, and I think I have broken about twenty barrels of dishes, upset stoves, and also broken up many sets of beautiful furniture, had my eyes blackened, both ankles sprained and many bruises, and I am still on the go. This is a great business."

Even Tom Mix offered his list of injuries. Of course, given his history for exaggeration, we might take this with a grain of salt, but enough of these incidents have been corroborated through other sources to certify that they're mostly authentic:

Sometimes I reckon I get to laughing over the fact that I quit being a sheriff to lead a quieter and less dangerous life. Making western pictures hasn't been exactly a quiet and peaceful life. I had three ribs broken one day in a shuffle; I had to have nine stitches taken in my head when somebody hit me with the wrong chair; a spur tore the whole side of my head open one day

*when I was doing a fight and the man's leg flew up; a horse crushed my toe;
I was filled plumb full of pieces of shot when a bomb exploded; I had a
tooth smashed in a scene one day.*

*Those are just a few of the things that happen. I've had to jump horses
thirty feet into a lake. I've had to jump them through plate glass windows
and from the roof of one building to another. I've ridden up and down fire
escapes. So sometimes I've thought it wasn't much of a change. As I heard
a kid say to his mother in a theater one day, when they were showing one
of my pictures, "If Tom and Tony aren't careful, they'll get seriously killed
one of these days."*

The members of the press were having such a gleeful time enumerating
the near-death experiences endured by the film actors and crews that they
were perhaps taken a bit by surprise when a bona fide tragedy actually
transpired during a shoot. It all fell on the innocent shoulders of a young
wannabe starlet who perhaps wasn't aware of—or chose to ignore—the
perils that awaited her when she joined the moving picture industry.

Grace McHugh was what we would call a modern, exciting woman.
She was born into the theatrical profession—her mother being a soubrette
with a theater company—and made her first appearance on stage at the
age of three. But she could also count as her achievements the skills of
expert horsewoman, accomplished swimmer and pioneering aviator. She
had already traveled extensively around the United States, Canada and
Mexico when, at the age of twenty-five, she thought she might dabble a
bit in the glamorous world of "the pictures." It would prove to be a tragic
decision. Grace would make only one film for the Colorado Motion Picture
Company, but her untimely death would affect the entire Rocky Mountain
film industry for years to come.

Across the Border was to be just the first of many films Miss McHugh would
make for the Colorado Motion Picture Company—an exciting story of
gunrunning across the Mexican border. She played the role of the bandit's
daughter. The principal photography had already been completed, but
one of the action scenes had been damaged in the development process.
Like the troopers they were, Grace and the company went back to re-
film the necessary footage, a hazardous river crossing on horseback. The
location was at the confluence of the Arkansas River and Grape Creek—
an area still categorized as being for "expert kayakers only" by present-day
recreation groups.

Grace McHugh adorns a postcard for the Colorado Motion Picture Company. "Miss McHugh, who was a pretty bit of blue eyed, black haired femininity as any one could wish to see." *Courtesy Royal Gorge Regional Museum & History Center.*

Grace McHugh seated on the buckboard for a shot in *Across the Border*. Sad to say, as is the case with so many films from this era, the only visual record we have of them is in production stills, such as this one, used to promote the film. *Courtesy Denver Public Library, Western History Department.*

The camera rolled, and Grace McHugh jauntily began the crossing. Unexpectedly, her horse stumbled, and she fell into the surging water, desperately holding on to her horse's reins. One of the crew rode to help her, but as director Otis B. Thayer would later recall, "She grabbed his hands so that he could do nothing. In his efforts to break her hold so that he could grab her the force of the water swept her away down stream. She held up her head and seemed to be floating nicely. I called 'bully for you, girlie, that's a brave girl, hold up and we'll get you.'"

Owen Carter, the company's assistant cameraman, jumped into the current alongside her. "He grabbed her and I saw him carry her to the sand bank. I hollered, 'thank God.'" The rest of the crew scrambled down the bank to give their assistance, but apparently Carter stumbled, for both he and Grace were thrown back into the river. By the time the men reached the sand bank, the two had vanished. There was no helping them now, and they were both carried away by the swift current. "The last that was seen of the

Grace McHugh and fellow performers in a promotional still for *Across the Border*. Unfortunately, the real danger was in the river at her feet rather than hiding in the bushes behind her. *The Moving Picture World* called the incident "[a]n unfortunate and rather unnecessary undertaking." *Courtesy Denver Public Library, Western History Department.*

ill-fated couple was when they sank beneath the surface of the river locked in the embrace of death."

And so, on that warm July day of 1914, Grace McHugh, a new star for the Colorado Motion Picture Company, and Owen Carter, up-and-coming cameraman, met their deaths in the rapids of the Arkansas River. Ironically, a previously conducted interview with Miss McHugh appeared in the paper the day the accident was reported: "Of course, to hold my job, I have to take many chances. I make it a rule to never get excited or to even think of the possible consequences. Often I have narrow escapes and frequently sustain physical injuries, but I never think of them at the time."

Outside Forces

It might be tempting to lay the demise of Colorado filmmaking—and, by inference, local filmmaking in general—at the feet of the tragic deaths of Grace McHugh and Owen Carter. And there are those who have said as much. But while darkly romantic and with a certain sense of poetic resonance, that would be overstating a situation that might more callously be regarded as an industrial accident—something that the unions and the Occupational Safety and Health Administration (OSHA) would begin to regulate in the coming years.

Tragic, yes. But enough to bring about the end of an industry? Not quite. The film folk paused for a moment and reflected. But as in the case of any death, after a month, even close friends adjust and move on. The Colorado Motion Picture Company did just that. It returned to production of its next project, one that had been started with Grace McHugh—bringing in a new actress and re-filming those scenes that had already been shot. But even at that, the company's fate echoed that of its predecessors—after this film, no other productions emerged from the small company, and it eventually closed its doors.

The tragedy of Grace McHugh and Owen Carter didn't decimate the fledgling Colorado motion picture industry (any more than Hollywood would let a little death get in the way of a good profit), although it did in many ways symbolize the death of filmmaking outside the emerging Hollywood system. There were much larger forces at work that would mark the demise of filmmaking as a significant business in Colorado, as well as local production throughout the United States in general.

That same year, 1914, the Strand Theater opened in New York City. The Strand is considered the first—or at least the first fully formed—of the great motion picture palaces. Within a few years, these majestic movie theaters would completely supplant the nickelodeons. *The Moving Picture World* took note of the theater's transcendent stature on the eve of its opening:

> *It is a million-dollar enterprise…One cannot stand in the center of the great theater and gaze at its marvels of beauty and comfort and light and color without feeling a thrill of joy. It does indeed mean something to the art and industry at large that a group of men of affairs have erected such a costly monument of their faith in the future of motion pictures.*
>
> *Here is a theater in which a master exhibitor…can do himself full justice. Here is a theater in which the film of quality will get its proper frame and housing…Here, in fine, is the ideal temple of the motion picture art.*

So what, you may ask, do such majestic theaters have to do with filmmaking in the middle of the country? The Strand was merely the first of a legion of larger movie theaters that would unseat the nickelodeon theaters within the space of a few years. They were built to showcase motion pictures of a more substantial nature than the short one-reel films that had been the mainstay of the film industry for more than a decade. And in that way, they were indicative of a larger movement that was transforming the film industry.

Interestingly, the movie that was chosen to consecrate this "temple of the motion picture art" was Colonel Selig's *The Spoilers*, at the time considered the epitome not only of film art but also of successful commercial film production. Its length was nine reels. Nine reels! That's more than two hours long. The Colorado Motion Picture Company's *Pirates of the Plains* ran just a little over half an hour. This was a significant change.

In the modern era, we are used to films running ninety minutes and longer. It's hard to imagine a time when lengthy feature films didn't even exist—a time when there was considerable controversy as to whether people would sit still long enough for an extended narrative. Film technique and structure had been steadily developing from the charming but creaky productions first released by Edison and the other fathers of film. Films continued to develop and evolve until they finally transformed into something completely new and different. The feature film was rapidly supplanting the one-reeler, and it needed a theater as grand as it was to show it.

The lobby of the Strand Theater at Forty-seventh Street and Broadway in New York City. "The general decorative scheme is ivory and gold with panels of embossed red plush, columns and balustrades of imitation marble, giving a beautiful effect under the lights. The seats are large and comfortable, covered with red plush." These were just a few of the choice words used by *The Moving Picture World* to describe this vanguard of the moving picture palace. The theater was demolished in 1987. *Courtesy Museum of the City of New York / Art Resource, New York.*

As noted by "Buck" Buckwalter (our old friend who had once organized free outdoor screenings for his one- and two-minute films), "The fact is, the ten-cent house and big feature programs have come to stay…and my prediction is that the next move will be to 25 cents, and then higher…to $1 per seat, and the higher the rate the more people are drawn, while the five-cent fellows stand around and say, 'It can't last.'"

The nickelodeons and their short one-reel films were already anachronisms. While the expanding film manufacturers in California were implementing lengthier and more elaborate productions, the Colorado companies were still gearing themselves to make what was becoming an antiquated format: short, straightforward westerns. The California companies were now staffing their facilities with entire Wild West shows, housed on the studio lots. Who could compete with that?

Movies were becoming big business and needed a central location, someplace where they could build a factory town. As productions became bigger and equipment became more specialized, they needed to have a major infrastructure supporting them.

In the same way that there wasn't much in the way of automobile manufacturing outside Detroit, movie production was becoming a scarce commodity outside Southern California. And Hollywood—that euphemism that was beginning to encompass all of Los Angeles—was attracting filmmakers. That same year in Hollywood, 1914, D.W. Griffith was filming *The Birth of a Nation*, the penultimate example of the Hollywood epic and still (adjusting for inflation and ticket pricing) one of the highest grossing films of all time. Also, Charlie Chaplin made his first film, beginning his spectacular rise to movie icon.

Another important event happened that year that would affect the film industry (along with everyone else), something called the Great War (or World War I as we know it now). In many respects, the war didn't personally affect the average American until many years later, when the United States actually entered the conflict. But it had an immediate effect on the film business. World War I served as the industry's wake-up call from the global economy. Overnight, a major portion of its revenue dropped as the European market was swallowed up in the smoke of war. Only the larger companies consolidating in California could absorb those losses.

And with these milestones came the close of the pre-Hollywood era of filmmaking as moviemakers gravitated toward the burgeoning California coastline. All of the actors, actresses, bit players, cameramen, writers, producers, crew and everyone else involved with filmmaking eventually found their way to Hollywood, too.

It had been a time of great transition in the young American film industry. In the two short decades since the birth of cinema, the Rocky Mountains had been home to hundreds of films. Only a small piece of this mammoth output has survived to the present day. These and all the endeavors of the motion picture pioneers offer us a glimpse of a vanishing America, a luminous era of growth and historical significance, of dreams and passions that still guide the imagination of this country, the collective memory of a nation captured on the ephemeral medium of film.

To Be Continued Elsewhere

As Hollywood can tell you (and usually does, over and over again), the end of one story only serves as the starting point for another. So, as the dust settled on filmmaking in the Rocky Mountains, it was already being stirred up elsewhere.

But what became of all the people—the producers, the directors, the actors and the entrepreneurs—who had passed through on their way to charting the course of an emerging industry? They had already been witness to the early years and exciting changes in that alluring mixture of art, commerce and public taste that film had become, and they still led prolific lives. But in many cases, the industry that they themselves had created was about to pass them by. Let's take a look at what became of these pioneers of the industry as the film industry moved forward—in many cases, without them.

Edison's legacy, of course, has proven to be the sturdiest. And although, as we've seen, he personally didn't actually invent the movies, he's given that recognition on a regular basis. And perhaps it's a somewhat deserved accolade since he truly was the catalyst for most of the technical progress made in those early years of the film industry. But while he was an indefatigable technician and a chillingly sharp businessman, he never quite understood the creative directions that movies were taking.

Like the tinkerer who continues fiddling with various aspects of his invention and loses sight of its ultimate purpose, he became perhaps overly focused on the technology. He continued to be at the forefront of film technology, and that, perhaps, was his problem. Technology, of course, was important and continues to be important in presenting moving entertainment. But without engaging content, there's really nothing to look at. Gilbert Anderson had this to say: "Old man Edison was a peculiar man; he didn't take any interest at all in the moving pictures. He took interest in the projection machine that made the pictures, or the camera, the patents. But after he got that all patented and all completed, he didn't care for the product, no more than he cared for the product of the electric light after it lit. But he was a smart old man. He was smarter than any of the birds in the Motion Picture Patents Company at that time."

Edison missed all the signs of the coming of the feature film and continued to produce catchy one-reelers of the sort that were rapidly becoming old-fashioned and dated. And his films slowly became bottom-of-the-barrel fare for most exhibitors. In early 1918, he shut his studio down and left the motion picture business for good. Despite his early experiments with sound, he hated the talkies. "The talkies have spoiled everything for me. There isn't any more good acting on the screen. They concentrate on the voice now and have forgotten how to act. I can sense it more than you because I am deaf. It's astounding how much more a deaf person can see."

In an ironic twist, Edison had his big head-on crash with reality when his Motion Picture Patents Company itself became the target of several lawsuits brought on by various independent filmmakers claiming an illegal monopoly, and eventually he was brought to court by the United States government. The antitrust suit dragged on for three years, from August 15, 1912, to October 1, 1915, when the Motion Picture Patents Company was found guilty. Frankly, it was a bit of an anticlimax since, by that time, most of the patents, issued years earlier in the 1890s, were expiring anyway.

As time went on, Edison became more circumspect and cultivated his status as the wise old sage. To the end, his motives were benevolent, or at least that's how he viewed them. As with a politician, though, it's sometimes hard to tell whether he's saying what he really feels or what he thinks he ought to feel. "I tell you, whatever you do for the proletariat pays. I am not done working for the proletariat...I am going to make the man that works in the ditch for $2.00 a day enjoy things which Louis XV could not have bought; yes, finer things than the French king ever saw or heard."

The legacies of the other filmmakers were not quite so immortal. "Buck" Buckwalter dropped out of the movie business rather early on. He kept in touch with Selig for quite some time after the latter set up his shop in California and, as near as we can tell, actually went to visit him on several occasions. Apparently, he didn't feel motivated to make the move to Selig's new digs. His last foray into moviemaking—and this is a good one—occurred in 1913 when he traveled to Panama to document the completion of the Panama Canal.

But like a little boy who can't keep his attention on one toy for too long, he began to lose interest in the motion picture; the novelty had just worn off for him, and Buckwalter, who had once been known in Colorado as "the moving picture man," turned his back on movies. But as his movie mania faded, a new technology captured his interest: sending voices through the air itself with radio. Soon, he and his equally energetic wife were broadcasting from their own home.

His days of local celebrity were passed, and his time of being the subject of local newspaper cartoons was behind him, but he was still well liked and respected. When he died, quietly, his obituary began with the appropriately quirky statement, "A pioneer in modernity died yesterday in Denver." This was 1930, and he was just sixty-two years old.

Fame is capricious. Just ask Broncho Billy Anderson. In the early teens, he was the biggest star to hit the silver screen. He acted in his own films, he directed them and he was the head of a major motion picture studio. Charlie Chaplin worked for *him*. But by 1916, he was out of the movie business and on his way to obscurity. Such is the way of celebrity.

After opening the production facility in California, the Essanay Company continued to flourish, quickly becoming one of the most successful film manufacturers in the country, with the Broncho Billy one-reelers playing constantly in theaters everywhere. Anderson was crowned "king of the movies." But even greater success was on the way for this progressive film company. In 1914, in a somewhat daring move, Anderson set his sights on signing Charlie Chaplin, who was just at the start of his meteoric rise to stardom. Chaplin had been hired by Keystone the year before at a conventional $150 per week. Now, one year later, the Little Tramp's success was so great that he was able to negotiate a shocking $1,250 per week from Gilbert Anderson. Back in the Chicago office, Anderson's partner George Spoor was aghast, but he recovered quickly as soon as Chaplin's films began making ludicrously huge sums of money. Essanay now had two major stars headlining its films: Broncho Billy Anderson and Charlie Chaplin. But Anderson's flamboyant business style was perhaps getting under Spoor's skin, and the papers were constantly running reports of each of them in turn denying rumors that they didn't get along—a sure sign that they didn't get along. Eventually, their whole business began to crumble from within.

"Buck" Buckwalter never lost his sense of fun and curiosity. Here he is late in life with his wife in their own personal radio broadcast center. Note the nice touch of a small cuckoo clock in the upper part of the photo. *Courtesy History Colorado.*

The first signs came when, after a year of successes, Charlie Chaplin's contract came due for renegotiation. George Spoor personally handled the negotiations and, after a somewhat weak-handed offer, let Chaplin go.

There are those who say that he had a more shrewd and perhaps underhanded business motive in mind. With Chaplin gone, the company's worth was now somewhat devalued, giving Spoor the opportunity to offer Anderson a diminished figure to buy his partner out of the company completely. In a move that tacitly confirmed the rumors of their ill will, Anderson accepted—some would say cutting off his nose to spite his face in a very public way. In an oddly brief squib in the February 16, 1916 edition of *The Moving Picture World*, under the curt title "Anderson Retires from Essanay Ownership," the paper announced, "Gilbert M. Anderson, secretary of the Essanay Company, has sold his stock interest to George K. Spoor, president of the concern...Mr. Anderson has not announced his future plans." In fact, his future plans were a little hazy at the time.

Anderson later recalled, "I sold Essanay out, and at that time I was well off financially, but not for long." Not for lack of trying. Within a year, he was back in the saddle, and the press triumphantly announced, "Following a year of inactivity in the motion picture industry G.M. ('Broncho Billy') Anderson will emerge from retirement…by presenting himself in a new six-reel feature photoplay called 'Humanity.'…'Broncho Billy' is again the central figure in a story wherein he portrays the cowboy, the character for which he is famed throughout the world." But George Spoor wasn't in the mood to play nice, and he blocked the release, claiming that Anderson no longer had the rights to the Broncho Billy character.

Anderson evaded that situation by producing a series of westerns in which he billed himself merely as the "famous creator of Broncho Billy" and released them through independent distributors. But they were mishandled and generally ignored by the moviegoing public. In any case, audience tastes had changed, and Anderson was never able to revive his career in a world demanding longer features with more depth in their characters. He went back to his first love, theater, and was somewhat successful, producing live stage productions, but he eventually opted for a quiet, secluded life away from the public eye.

At the time of his highest fame, a reviewer had declared that "like the British drum beat, which rolls around the world, Broncho Billy never ceases to prance upon the movie stage. At any time, some place on this earth, Bill is spurring his mustang across the screen. He never quits."

But like a phantom or a dream that blazes gloriously in your conscious mind, once the dream is over, the image fades and is gone. He was out of the public eye for so long that most people thought he was dead, at least those who even remembered him. Then, in the late 1950s, a Hollywood reporter, nosing around for a good story, stumbled on the fact that Anderson was quite alive. After a number of profile pieces began appearing in the press, he was back in the industry's eye again. Finally, he was given a special Oscar in 1958.

He was delighted at the renewed recognition. "I loved to make these pictures. I thought that was my life, as long as they were good. Finally, I got kind of tired of it, you know. I don't know whether I got tired of the admiration or the foolishness of it—because I never take it seriously, which some of them do—and you should. Maybe that was my downfall, that I didn't take it seriously and finally got out of it, went in, as they say, to moth balls."

George Spoor, Anderson's partner at Essanay, had to face the reality of the simultaneous loss of the studio's two most bankable stars: Broncho Billy and Charlie Chaplin. Initiating sweeping changes, he shut down the

Gilbert "Broncho Billy" Anderson proudly displays his special Oscar in 1958. "I feel 30 years younger. No more mothballs for me." *Courtesy Niles Essanay Silent Film Museum.*

Niles plant as soon as Gilbert Anderson was gone and began bankrolling a number of technological advances in filmmaking—notably a widescreen 3D process that he called Natural Vision. It was a unique process in that it didn't require special glasses for viewing but rather was projected on two screens simultaneously, one translucent screen in front of one regular opaque screen. It's a little difficult to determine the success of the results as most press accounts of the time are tainted with promotional hyperbole.

In 1923, the *New York Times* announced that "the moving picture world is to be thrilled by a new discovery, the capture of the third dimension. It is the natural vision picture, claims its inventor, George K. Spoor...The screen will fill the proscenium arch of the largest theatre and will hold the most grandiose production. On it, through the stereopticon process, the actors are given form and body, the background is given depth, the whole picture gains atmosphere." But Spoor could never quite get the process to work as well as advertised. At various intervals over the next few years, he would make periodic announcements heralding its ultimate perfection being finally at hand. Whatever amount of perfection it may have achieved, it never achieved commercial success.

Spoor spent the remainder of his professional life obsessed with this project. He received a special Oscar in 1948 for his pioneering efforts in film. But he probably would rather have had a projecting system that was accepted by the film industry.

Colonel Selig also saw his fortunes wane as the 1910s moved forward. Although he continued to advance new ideas—he originated the concept of the cliffhanger serial with *The Adventures of Kathlyn* in 1913—he was not so forward-thinking in other areas. Despite having taken the commercially risky move of releasing a nine-reel film, 1914's *The Spoilers*, shortly after, he was one of the first to decry the advent of feature-length movies. He declared, "That the single reel photo-drama is the keystone of the motion picture industry becomes more apparent daily. Patrons of the film drama want their programs as diversified as possible. A program offering four or more productions is more apt to please an entire audience than is a program offering one photo-play of four or five reels...The ordinary, so-called feature play will not satisfy, and has a tendency to injure the motion picture business."

Increasingly, many of his films were jungle adventures, and he found himself caring for so many animals that in 1915 he opened his own zoo, the Selig Zoo, which became somewhat of a public attraction in its own right. He'd rent his animals to other studios for their films, and Hollywood lore has it that one of the many MGM lions filmed over the years for use as its identifying logo was, in fact, from Selig's zoo.

Though no longer a leading player in the film industry, he stayed in the game. He was able to finance his later years not in splendor but not in poverty by bartering film rights to the many book and story properties he'd purchased

Other people may have had children or grandchildren to dote on, but Colonel Selig had a zoo full of animals! Today, the Los Angeles Zoo benefits from a donor organization called the Selig Legacy Society in honor of the great animal lover. *Courtesy Margaret Herrick Library, Academy of Motion Picture Arts and Sciences.*

in his younger years. In fact, he became a real wheeler-dealer in intellectual properties, stating, "There is just another bit of Selig history of which I am proud, the early acquisition of film rights to books and plays when authors and playrights [*sic*] thought it a joke, albeit a well paid one, to receive fifty dollars for the screen rights of a novel or stage play. I do not claim to be the first to see the day coming when there would be an overwhelming demand for the published work but I was the first to go out and pay real money—at least it was considered real then—for the commodity no producer had any use for at that time."

He was honored with a special award from the Academy of Motion Picture Arts and Sciences in 1948 as one of "the small group of pioneers whose belief in a new medium, and whose contributions to its development, blazed the trail along which the motion picture has progressed, in their lifetime, from obscurity to world-wide acclaim." He died just four months later in his Hollywood home, a respected and not entirely forgotten man.

A few years before his death, the *Motion Picture Herald* ran a retrospective of Selig's career. After spending a day with the octogenarian, the Hollywood editor reported, "It is my impression he'd be a tough fellow to trim in a poker game."

Of all these early filmmakers, Tom Mix had the most colorful and "Hollywoodized" career. As Broncho Billy's career was fading and Selig's studio was waning, Tom was just hitting his stride. Because the Selig studio was cutting its budgets, he moved on to Fox, where he embellished and perfected the over-the-top rambunctiousness that was his trademark.

Throughout the 1920s, his oversized grin and equally oversized ten-gallon hat became genial fixtures in movie theaters across the country and around the world. But as the '20s ramped down—and as Mix's stunt injuries ramped up—Tom was looking for a way to graciously retire from the movies. The Great Depression, alimony for several ex-wives and his own high-on-the-hog lifestyle prevented that. He made a series of sound pictures and appeared in—and even bought—a Wild West circus. He made it back to Colorado to film only one more time for *The Great K&A Train Robbery* in 1926.

In 1933, the *Tom Mix Ralston Straight Shooters* radio show (sponsored by Ralston-Purina) debuted, each week chronicling the adventures of Tom Mix—or rather, the adventures of a licensed Tom Mix. Mix himself never appeared on the show. He found it easier to authorize his name and character, while he was portrayed on air by another actor—actually, in the long run of the show, by four succeeding actors.

It's a little hard to figure exactly, but it's estimated that Mix made anywhere from $6 to $10 million during his twenty-six-year film career. Adjusting for inflation, this would translate to more than $160 million in today's money. He had a lot of things to spend that money on. In addition to his previous wives, he maintained several extravagant homes, including one that had his name installed in neon on the roof (great for any passing planes). He even had special tires made for his fleet of cars with his initials "TM" embossed on them so they'd leave a track when he drove over soft ground or mud.

He lived extravagantly, and he died extravagantly. On a clear October day in 1940, he was driving along Arizona State Route 79 between Tucson and Phoenix. In the back seat of his convertible, he had an aluminum case filled with money, traveler's checks and jewelry. Witnesses say that he was traveling at more than eighty miles per hour when he swerved to avoid some construction barriers and rolled his car, ending up overturned in a gully. The aluminum case flew forward and struck him on the back of his head, killing him instantly. In a flamboyant final touch that Mix no doubt would have approved of, when emergency personnel pulled his body from the car, his suit was clean, his body was unscathed and no blood was spattered anywhere.

Mix once spoke of the passing of the "West of Yesterday," with its herds of cattle, its ranches and its wild towns. His comments could have been an epitaph for himself: "With them, has gone the cowboy of the old days, the most picturesque figure this nation ever produced—the cowboy sitting so loosely and gracefully in his saddle, with his bronzed face and keen eyes, his bright handkerchief and big chaps. I hope the people of this country won't soon forget him, and I reckon they won't, for no one has been more splendidly sung in song and story and poetry." Interestingly, Mix's radio program ran for a full ten years after his death.

Otis B. Thayer stayed in Colorado for quite some time, really trying to make a go of building a film industry on the Front Range. As one company would fold, he and his band of fellow filmmakers would start another, going through film companies like a bartender goes through bottles of bourbon. After the Cheyenne Motion Picture Company, Columbine Film Company and the Colorado Motion Picture Company, there was the Pikes Peak Motion Picture Company, the National Film Company of Colorado and Art-O-Graf. None of them seemed to stick. So, like many in the film business, he eventually moved to California and worked on second- and third-string projects until his death in 1935.

A peculiar coda was added to his life story late in his career. Under the headline "Thayer Nearly Drowned," *The Moving Picture World* reported that he had been directing a Colorado film in 1920 when he "waded out into the flooded Gunnison River the other day to find a location. In his enthusiasm he waded too far, and suddenly found himself sinking in quicksand, and only the assistance of other members of the company saved him." I'm sure the irony did not escape him.

And what of the western itself? What became of that reliable genre? The western was the durable workhorse that lasted from decade to decade, reinventing itself, rewriting its own history and always resurrecting itself as the perennial reflection of its time—retaining its standard characters and its own grim determination. But sometime in the 1960s, it just seemed to peter out. How could it just vanish?

The simple answer is that it didn't. It transformed itself completely, almost unrecognizably, into the science fiction film. The appearance may have changed, but the underlying concepts remain the same. Gene Roddenberry, creator of the resilient *Star Trek* franchise, famously described his creation as a "*Wagon Train* to the stars." (*Wagon Train* was a western television series of the early '60s.)

I don't know about you, but I'm always suspicious of anything that has to tell you it's high class. Art-O-Graf was a film company set up with Otis Thayer in 1919, with offices in Steamboat Springs, Colorado. *Courtesy Denver Public Library, Western History Department.*

To be sure, science fiction had been a popular subject of films practically from the beginning, going back as far as George Méliès's much-celebrated *A Trip to the Moon* of 1902. But it was hardly a standard genre. The high-spirited *Flash Gordon* films of the 1930s were the acknowledged inspiration for the reimagined sci-fi films of the 1970s, but the transfer wasn't exact. The simple, straightforward storylines of the earlier science fiction films became purposefully, even self-consciously, mythic in scope—similar to the philosophical approach that western films had been taking. And many of the themes and formulas of the western were absorbed into the sci-fi epic of today. When the seemingly limitless expanses of the prairies and mountains became confined by the automobile, the cellphone and our modern sense of distance, the stories moved to the limitless expanses of outer space. A vast, symbolic prairie has been replaced by a vast, symbolic interstellar space. The faceless Indians have become the faceless aliens. The power-mad villains, the lawless land, the moral ambiguity of the hero—it's all there. It's all part of the same myth.

Very late in his life, Broncho Billy Anderson, the last survivor of the lot of them, said, "You wanted to know if I think Westerns have changed. Well, of course they've changed; any naked eye can see that they've changed. They're getting more stupendous, and they're getting more detail, more acting, but I don't think they've changed in entertainment. I think the Westerns of the days gone by entertained the public that they had just as well as these pictures entertain the public today. But they didn't give them the production."

Perhaps deep down, our new movies of today really have nothing more to offer than what the old movies gave us in story, plot, character or entertainment. It's just that the new productions have become larger, more expensive and more sprawling. Does that make them better? Or just "more stupendous"?

PART II

BEFORE, DURING AND AFTER

B ack in the great, Golden Age of Hollywood, a night at the movies would not only involve a feature film but would also begin with a number of short subjects: cartoons, newsreels, documentaries and such. This book reverses that order: we started with the feature film, and since the more curious reader might be interested in a few more details, I've got some short subjects ready to augment the enjoyment of this story about the early filmmakers.

Essentially, this is a look at the world in which William Selig, Gilbert Anderson, Thomas Edison and Tom Mix grew up, the world that affected their thinking, desires and aspirations. It was the world in which they lived—a world that, to a certain extent, they created, or at least had a pretty big hand in creating. It was the world that ultimately became their legacy.

Now, I'm not talking about every cultural influence of the times—the clothes, the food, the modes of transportation, the books, city life, country life and all those things that make a world complete. Of course, all these affected the growth of the movies. But that would be a separate and rather large book in itself. This is merely a glimpse at the world of public entertainments that most directly influenced and were influenced by the movies and their development.

Before the movies were the movies, there was already a vast amount of popular amusements that would affect the growth of the film industry and fashion the expectations of an entertainment-hungry populace for the medium that would become the cinema. This was the world of entertainment into which the filmmaking industry was born—in essence, the world of the motion picture industry before it even existed.

Then, once the movies became less newfangled and more common, they began their transformation into the cinema that we know today. The audience was an important part of that because the interface between moviemaker and moviegoer was the movie theater—something of a new concept in itself. This was the world of the filmmaking industry from the point of view of the end user, the theater patron.

But when the movies left Colorado for Hollywood, was it the end? A quick time jump forward into the present reveals that there's a bit of a reversal going on. Like most industries today, there's a trend to decentralization, and even moviemaking itself is now being outsourced. What follows includes a look at how the filmmaking world of the early pioneers eventually became our world—filmmaking today in the Rocky Mountains. And it's far different from what you've read so far.

Here then, is a brief look into the world of film and the world of our filmmakers in the days before, during and after the pioneering decades of the industry.

Backstory to the Cinema

You have to imagine yourself footloose and fancy-free in the latter part of the nineteenth century. It's a Friday night, you've got a little disposable cash in your pocket and you're looking for something to do. There's precious little in the way of entertainment at home—no television, no online surfing and certainly no smartphones—so you definitely want to go out. Your choices might include getting a few drinks at the local saloon, hanging out at a pool hall, perhaps taking in a boxing match, going to the theater for a popular melodrama, maybe spending a little time at the vaudeville or something that we, sitting smugly in the twenty-first century, might not think of: a magic lantern show. Yes, a *magic lantern* show—basically, a slide presentation. And again, before you get too smug, listen to all that this entailed.

You see, when we talk about the early days of cinema, it's easy to get lost in the whole argument of who invented what and when and who did it first and who gets the preeminent bragging rights for which. Though interesting to track, all these claims lose sight of what movies really are. Though the motion picture was certainly a technological innovation, its primary impact on us has been as a commercial and cultural phenomenon. And the whole thing sprang up right in the middle of an already vibrant industry devoted to entertaining the public with projected images. "What?" you say. "I thought the movies just popped out of nowhere and surprised everyone. That's what had everyone so bowled over, isn't it?"

Not exactly. As they say, most forms of public amusement emerge from those preceding them. So, too, did movies emerge from an already existing cultural experience. And believe it or not, the history of pre-movies goes back a long way.

The first really successful magic lantern show was, in fact, a bit of a multimedia extravaganza that took place back in the 1790s in post-revolutionary France. It was a show called *Phantasmagoria*, and it played in an abandoned chapel, terrifying audiences with projections of spirits that appeared to travel around the room and grow in size, thanks to mobile projectors and special lenses. The images were painted on glass slides and projected onto a variety of different surfaces—including gauze and (literally) smoke and mirrors. The show would bring back icons of history and recently deceased heroes of the Revolution. Now, audiences weren't stupid. They knew that these weren't actual spirits but rather clever manipulations. Perhaps too clever. The theater was shut down temporarily when someone in authority (who perhaps wasn't as bright as the rest) thought that the proprietor might be clever enough to actually reanimate the recently decapitated King Louis XVI.

These images were hand-drawn and hand-painted onto the glass. But when the technology of photography advanced to the point that photographs could be printed on the slides and projected onto a screen, a whole new industry was born. These projected images created quite a stir at their debut at London's Crystal Palace Exhibition of 1851. This was the first time a real image had been projected at life size (or larger!), and a critic of the time marveled that "the result is as near an approach to perfection as we can imagine…We have now before us a series of these magic-lantern slides… and we feel bound to declare that their delicacy and the perfection of the details cannot be overstated."

That did it. In towns and cities all over Europe and America, audiences were rushing to see these marvelous images from the magic lanterns—or, as they were often called, stereopticons, which, despite the multidimensional name, did not project 3D images. A stereopticon was a group of lantern projectors stacked two or even three across. By dissolving from one projector to the next, the operator achieved a smooth transition between slides. Quaintly enough, the operator of such a device was called a stereoptician.

Audiences could go to these "illustrated lectures" and feel not only entertained but also educated, being transported to places and times they'd never been to. Exotic views of Japan and Norway, English history, French history, sacred scenes, famous people, noteworthy sculpture and more—all were available through the enchantments of the magic lantern. Usually, these were narrated by trained lecturers, those who held the (often self-

The Victorian worldview brought to life by the magic lantern show. "By magnifying these new slides through the magic lantern, the representation is nature itself again," enthused the *Art-Journal* of London in 1851. *Author's collection.*

proclaimed) title of "traveler, explorer, lecturer and author." The travel lecture, in particular, was quite popular—and probably more entertaining than the last PowerPoint presentation you sat through.

As the market expanded, companies were formed expressly for the manufacture of projectors and accompanying slides for commercial magic lantern exhibitions. The average exhibitor could buy the slides—including the printed lecture notes—and present them himself. Lantern slide projection became a booming business. By the mid-1890s, a typical catalogue offered the option of more than 100,000 slides to choose from. As one supplier rejoiced, "The question of profit in a well managed Stereopticon Exhibition is one which admits of but one answer. This form of entertainment is exceedingly popular among all classes, and when the proper means are employed to bring it before the public it cannot fail to be highly remunerative."

This was a full evening's entertainment. And it was clearly entertaining to the audiences of the time. As one spectator rhapsodized, "No less than fifty magnificent views were thrown upon the screen, and many of them were so beautifully colored that the audience repeatedly broke into applause."

In addition to factual locations and subjects, presentations of fictional stories and dramas were very popular. You could see "Comic Tales" and children's stories such as *Dick Whittington*, *Tom Thumb* and semi-fictional recreations of historic events such as *Sir Isaac Newton and the Apple*. Of course, the big literary hits also found their way into illustrated presentations: Edgar Allan Poe, Henry Wadsworth Longfellow and William Shakespeare. The biggest of them all was *Uncle Tom's Cabin*. It was sort of the *Gone With the Wind* or *Star Wars* of the time—you could always rely on it to bring in a crowd.

Here are just a few of the images available for a presentation called *The Gossips*, a twelve-slide "lecture" available to exhibitors for six dollars, with narrative notes included:

- *Mrs. Chatterbox and Mary Dawdle enjoying a quiet gossip*
- *They are separated by a man with a barrow*
- *The town-crier divides them…*
- *The military school marches past…*
- *A flock of geese pass unheeded between them…*
- *A pig gets tripped up between them*
- *Thunder and lightning ends the conversation*

These were complete programs: a trained actor (or two or more) could be hired to recite the narrative, often supplemented by a musical accompaniment, along with sound effects. In short, it was pretty much a well-produced evening's entertainment.

And finally, in 1894, a feature-length "picture play" called *Miss Jerry* made its debut, prepared specifically for stereopticon presentation. This two-hour program was the invention of writer Alexander Black and presented a photographed fictional story posed in slides by actors in authentic locations. "Primarily my purpose," he said, "was to illustrate art with life." The drama was presented as a series of sequential slides, and it was "filmed" using a locked-down, carefully registered camera so that the background would remain stationary while the actors would appear in changed positions from slide to slide. When the program was presented, live actors would voice individual parts with a musical accompaniment. While not intended to represent smooth, fluid motion, the slides would change at the rate of about four per minute—not much compared to our current twenty-four-frames-per-second film, but it did give a sense of movement. Alexander Black viewed his invention as a combination of art and craft: "[N]ot only could I pass from one fictitious scene to another, but I could introduce the backgrounds

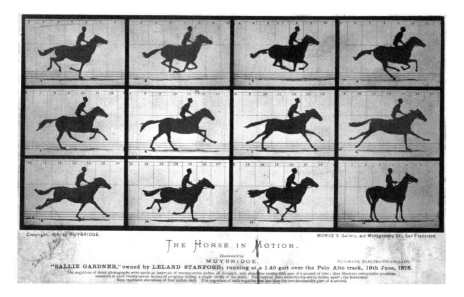

This is a postcard displaying the photos that Eadweard Muybridge took of a horse in motion. Imagine separating each individual image out and projecting it sequentially onto a screen, and you have the Zoopraxiscope. The photos would cycle from image one through eleven and then begin the sequence again. The twelfth image shows the horse in repose and would not have been included in a motion sequence. *Courtesy Library of Congress, Prints and Photographs Division.*

of real life, as I have done in several instances, bringing the living characters of my fictitious action against the actual life of the city."

Miss Jerry anticipated by twenty years the principles of story structure, scene presentation, continuity, sequencing and establishing shots that would eventually dominate motion pictures—well before the time that movies could have handled anything nearly so sophisticated. As film journalist Terry Ramsaye later proclaimed, "This event of 1894 seems quite as remarkable as though the apple had come into being before the tree."

Meanwhile, of course, there had been patchy attempts at projecting *moving* images on the screen before the invention of the cinématographe and the Vitascope. The most noteworthy was the Zoopraxiscope, created by Eadweard Muybridge. In one of the great tales of motion picture lore, the story goes that in 1872, Leland Stanford, then governor of California, hired photographer Muybridge to create a series of photos of a horse galloping in order to settle a wager he had made that all four of a horse's hooves would, at a certain point, be off the ground. This, by the way, was an issue of considerable debate at the time. Muybridge lined up a series of cameras in a row with trip wires attached to each, triggered as the horse galloped by. In a stunning coup, the individual photos settled the bet in Stanford's favor.

But in order to give the proper sense of movement to the series, Muybridge created a method of viewing the individual images sequentially, giving the illusion of actual motion. This was the Zoopraxiscope, a device that projected the pictures in succession. The images were copied onto a flat glass disc that was affixed behind the lens of a projector and rotated synchronously with a slotted shutter mechanism. The result was startlingly lifelike but limited, by the size of the disc, to cyclical movement. Full, sustained movement remained trapped for a good while inside the little peep show Kinetoscope box.

So, given all this, it's really not so much a wonder *that* the projected motion picture was created, but rather *why* it took so long in the first place. In any case, this was the world of entertainment already available to the soon-to-be moviegoing audience on the eve of the creation of the cinématographe, and a lot of the presentation techniques hung around into the movies.

Motion pictures would continue to be a simple novelty, until the day that the nickelodeon changed the face of entertainment for good.

A Trip Around the World for a Nickel

Cinema when you want it, where you want it, was hardly a concept that would have had any resonance with the moviegoing public of the early twentieth century. At this time, when people were just beginning to realize the concept of taking the time to sit down and watch a movie, the experience was quite a bit different than that of today, even discounting the fact that we moderns have about a dozen alternate ways to view our content, between television and computers and smartphones and all.

For the first few years of their existence, films were something of a stepchild in the entertainment world. They'd tag along to be shown as part of a vaudeville lineup, they'd appear at county fairs or traveling circuses in what were called "black tent shows" and they'd even be part of lecture presentations in rented halls or churches across the country. And then something changed. The nickelodeon arrived. It began modestly enough in 1905 on a quiet street in Pittsburgh on a quiet evening, but the reception wasn't quiet at all. Within a few months of its opening, the trade paper *The Moving Picture World* heralded its arrival:

> *There is a new thing under the sun—at least new within a short period of time—and entirely new in the sense that the public is waking up to what it means.*
>
> *It is the 5-cent theater.*
>
> *The nickel place of amusement made its appearance with no greater blare of trumpets than the noise of its phonograph horn and the throaty persuasions of its barker. It came unobtrusively, in the still of night. It is*

*multiplying faster than guinea pigs, and within a few months has attained
to that importance where we may no longer snub it as one of the catch-
pennies of the street.*

The movie theater was here to stay. And as we've already noted, its
influence was enormous. It's all well and good to talk about the importance
of the nickelodeon in the abstract sense, but to really feel its impact, we
have to look at the whole situation on a much more personal level. What
was it like to see a movie during the infancy of the industry? What was
it like to go into a theater that was designed—of all things—as a place
strictly to view movies?

Nickelodeons, once they established themselves, came in all shapes
and sizes. It was an eclectic bag. Some could be pretty shabby, but some
were fancy, with thoughtfully designed accoutrements for the comfort and
enjoyment of their patrons. And if you could step inside one today, there
would be a lot you'd recognize but also a lot you wouldn't—some things that
might even perplex you completely. But generally speaking, once the first
nickelodeon opened in 1905, movie theaters were pretty much on their way
to taking the general form that we know today.

At the finer nickelodeons, the magic began before you even walked inside
the door with dreamlike façades that began your transportation to the land
of make-believe right at the doorstep. In 1908, our good friend "Buck"
Buckwalter noted a trend for extravagance in movie theater appointments,
particularly "one place in Buffalo where $25,000 was spent in putting in an
onyx front that extended up two stories, and the interior was more gorgeously
fitted than any regular playhouse in the city. Chicago can show the same."
The more ambitious theater manager could build an ornate façade himself,
but for the more casual manager, façades made from terra cotta, wood,
onyx and more—complete with projector room and ticket booth—could
be purchased prefabricated from catalogues designed to cater to the up-
and-coming business. And to make it even easier, the 1908 Sears, Roebuck
catalogue offered "Complete Outfits for 5-Cent Theaters, Traveling
Exhibitors, Street Advertising, Lodge Work, Church Entertainments, Public
Schools at the Very Lowest Prices."

It wasn't long before the more regally appointed theaters began to eclipse
the cheap storefronts. *The Nickelodeon*, a trade magazine for theater owners,
noted that, "The time is past when any man can turn a barn into a theater
by painting an arch over the door and cutting a hole for the ticket-seller's

This ad from *The Moving Picture World* promoted theater fronts for sale. A number of major studios of today began as the creations of people who started out in the storefront theater business, including Warner Bros., Twentieth Century Fox and Paramount Pictures. *Courtesy Norlin Library, University of Colorado.*

window. As a matter of fact, a good many of the 'legitimate' play-houses must bow to the superior beauty of some neighboring picture theater."

Once inside, the layout of the theaters was a little more straightforward. The first thing you'd notice, of course, would be the large screen occupying the wall at the far end. In the very early days of storefront theaters, this would be nothing more than a canvas stretched over a frame or, in some cases, merely pinned to the wall. But the tackiness of that sort of a setup quickly became obvious. An instruction manual of the times offered a more aesthetic option: "Any wall screen or drop curtain screen may be treated by a coat of paint containing finely-divided aluminum dust, or finely-powdered glass, or the curtain may be painted with any sticky paint and the metallic dust or powdered glass thrown or blown upon it and, when the sticky paint dries, a glittering surface will remain upon the screen producing what is known as the *metal-surfaced* screen."

A higher-class establishment might have a "mirror screen," which consisted of a large sheet of plate glass, mirrored on the back and ground to a smooth ground-glass finish on the front, resulting in a gratifying degree of luminance in the projected image.

The seating arrangements also varied from theater to theater. The smaller theaters (those seating one hundred to two hundred patrons) would often have seats of the kitchen chair variety. Not so bad when you think that in the early years of the era, you might only be sitting for as long as fifteen minutes. But the finer establishments that began to spring up (seating three hundred or more) would usually have cushioned opera seats. Larger, classier theaters would have ushers and be equipped with sloping floors to aid in better sightlines to the screen. This would raise the eye level of patrons in the rear seats above those in the front—a sort of primitive version of stadium seating. One more thing, and this is very important: the projectionist's booth would be lined with sheet iron to mitigate the potentially disastrous effects in the theater of the extremely flammable nitrate film then in use.

The concession stand wouldn't make its way into theater lobbies until well into the 1930s, so popcorn was not yet a staple of the moviegoer's diet. But there was always the eager "candy butcher," a boy who would make his way up and down the aisle with his basket of sweet treats to sell. The more clever vendor would enhance sales by making his routine as entertaining as the movies, with such time-honored expressions as, "Don't be afraid to buy it; it's worth the money," "The young man takes two packages because the young lady knows it's good," "Every package guaranteed to send you home fat and happy," or, "After you eat it, if you don't like it, give it back and I'll refund the nickel." And once the show had started, he might offer, "Keep your eyes on the pictures and hand me your money." In rare instances, a theater manager might have installed a candy vending machine near the entrance of the theater.

Once you sat down in your seat, the show was ready to begin. At the beginning of the nickelodeon era, shows ran pretty much continuously. Shortly after the craze began, *The Moving Picture World* described a typical presentation:

> *Each "performance" lasts fifteen minutes. At the end of each a sign is thrown from the cinematograph on the canvas announcing that those who came late may stay for the next "performance."*
>
> *Often they stay for several. After they find out that nobody cares and that they can stay all day and far into the night and bring their lunch if they want to, they leave, disappointed because nobody tried to get the best of them.*
>
> *They are great places for the foot-sore shopper, who is not used to cement sidewalks, to rest; and it took the aforesaid foot-sore shoppers about one minute to find this out. It is much more comfortable than to take street-car rides to rest, and they don't have to pay the return nickel.*

The typical performance schedule changed, however, as the movie industry became more established. The shows became longer and more elaborate, and management went to great lengths to clear the theaters after each performance.

All had music of some sort, even if it was only an automatic piano. At this time, even the larger houses in the big cities would have no more than a piano, a drummer, perhaps a "sound artist" (for audio effects) or violin and a singer. It wasn't until later in the silent era that larger orchestras (some of symphonic size) began accompanying movies.

And a real staple of any nickelodeon show was the illustrated song. These were magic lantern slide presentations of popular songs of the day, and just like MTV and VH1 of recent years, they were essentially marketing tools for music publishers ("the song on our program is for sale at our ticket window"). There would be maybe ten to fifteen slides illustrating various key points of the melody and then a chorus slide with words would encourage audience participation as a sort of singalong. The usual procedure was to alternate a one-reel film with an illustrated song.

Denver became such a movie town that an area on Curtis Street became known as "Moving Picture Row." Can you imagine what fun it would have been to walk down this luminous street when this photo was taken in 1913? *Courtesy Denver Public Library, Western History Department.*

The smaller theaters would have perhaps three reels and two songs for each performance to make up a one-hour program. They'd operate each day of the week, offering four shows a night in the evenings, with added performances on Saturday. High-class theaters would offer more elaborate programs, and especially in larger cities, a greater number of performances necessitated that they hire two shifts. A management expert of the time outlined the rather frenetic behind-the-scenes schedule of a major theater:

The order of the program is as follows: The show starts with a few announcement slides; then the first motion-picture operator puts on the first film picture. As the end of the film picture approaches the stereopticon operator stands ready and projects the song title upon the tailpiece of the film, the pianist opens the introduction to the song as the title appears and the song follows without a second of lost time. At the close of the song, the second motion-picture operator stands ready and begins projection at a signal from the stereopticon operator, the last slide of the song dissolving into the title of the next film picture. In the same manner the screen continues without interruption of projection into the second song and then into the third film picture by the first projection operator. At the close of the third film picture the lights are turned on, the crowd is allowed a few minutes for passing out and in, the candy man makes a trip, and the program is repeated. The house is "dark" about fifty minutes for the program of three pictures and two songs, and is "light" for about five minutes for the intermission.

Programs would change two or three times per week. In smaller towns, the programs would usually change on a daily basis—that's right, a different film lineup each day. So, the schedule offered something like the variety you'd find on television these days. And that's why Colonel Selig, Gilbert Anderson and George Spoor, along with dozens of other movie manufacturers of the time, were busting their guts to keep this market filled.

From the smallest, shabbiest nickelodeon in a rural community to the most ornate bastion in the city to the most nondescript working-class theater in the borough, people were flocking to the movies. "Going to the movies" entered the language as a concept.

The theaters became larger and more lavish as the years wore on, until finally the whole thing culminated in the opening of New York's Strand in 1914—the theater that heralded the extraordinary age of the moving picture palace. The Strand, located in Times Square, was designed as a place in which to spend quality time and watch a lengthier production. With its inviting seats, expansive lobby and draperied recesses, it was practically like entering an opera house.

This was the moment. Films were becoming big business. Very big business, indeed.

Making a Movie Ain't What It Used to Be

I t's been more than one hundred years since the events of this book took place—one hundred years since the early moviemakers passed through the Rocky Mountains seeking those extraordinary and exhilarating locations. The original pioneers of the movies have come and gone, and several generations separate us from the days when movies were an electrifying new art form to be discovered and developed by a pioneering young band of enthusiasts. And if Colonel Selig and Gilbert Anderson and all the others could see the film business today, they would no doubt be profoundly amazed.

A century ago, the industry coalesced in the hills and valleys around Los Angeles, and aside from the rare and well-publicized location shoot over the years, it stayed there. Hollywood was a fortress of the motion picture factory, and it seemed it would stand forever.

Then, everything changed. Entire volumes and multivolume volumes have been written about the rise and fall and transformation of the Hollywood studio system. But we don't have that much space here. So, if we were to do a quick time zap of the last century in the American film business, it would look like this.

The Hollywood studios ran a financially tight ship in that first half of the twentieth century, controlling all links in the chain, not just the making of the movies but also their distribution and exhibition in the movie houses across America. They literally owned (or controlled) the motion picture theaters that were showing their films, and through this "vertical integration," the studios had it all.

Then, just like the Motion Picture Patents Company before them, an antitrust suit was brought against the studios. In 1948, in a case known as *United States v. Paramount Pictures, Inc.*, the Supreme Court ordered the studios to divest themselves of their distribution and exhibition arms. It was bad timing from the standpoint of the studios because it happened just as the onslaught of television hit. With their monopolistic edge lost, the studios began to uncomfortably downsize.

They became completely different animals with completely different business models. They couldn't afford to keep the large staff of managers, technicians and creatives on the payroll, and as they cut back, their function became more that of being financial backers of independent producers. Gone were the days when movie studios could initiate a project and develop it using their in-house staff.

They sold off most of their precious back lots years ago. Those that remain have been downsized and are available as rentable production facilities offering office space, production support services and sound stages on a fee basis to independent producers. And if you've got the right kind of cash behind you, you can even rent a studio for your next big event (the same way you'd rent a hall, but with a little more attendant glamour).

Most films these days are put together as individual, stand-alone projects. That's like assembling an entire new business for each film that gets produced. Without the engulfing arms of the studio, everything now has to be outsourced, making it incredibly difficult to get a film produced. It would be like hand-building a single new and original car and trying to find a market for it.

Working under the studio system may have been like working in a sausage factory, but it had its advantages. For one, you had the resources of the entire factory at your disposal. Nowadays, each new film project has to create its own sausage factory around itself. That's why filmmakers are always looking for a bargain on production resources. Even at rental rates, Hollywood studios don't come cheap. Eventually, someone thought, "Maybe I can find this cheaper somewhere else."

In 1997, Canada took the innovative step of marketing itself to film producers as an inexpensive alternative to shooting in Hollywood by offering financial incentives to make movies "north of the border." It worked. Hollywood's deep infrastructure and concentration of talent began to lose some of its allure when confronted with cheaper costs. And in an atmosphere of more mobile production in general, the incentives began to siphon film production out of California. Well, once the pie is cut, everyone wants a slice, so very soon other locations began to offer incentives, from tax credits to cash rebates to loan guarantees. Other states and other countries began to lure film production to their locales and created film commissions to scrutinize the problem—all of them working hard to get production out of California and into their locales. The business has become so ferociously competitive that even the State of California has initiated production incentives of its own to lure business back home and curb what's called "runaway production."

So, unlike the days of yore, the question of shooting in a location like Colorado is not answered so much by the beauty or appropriateness of the location as by what incentives are being offered. Colorado created the very first state film commission in the country, opening its doors in 1969, predating the current trend by decades. (In 2003, funding for the commission was cut from the state budget but was reinstated in 2009 as the Colorado Office of Film, Television and Media.) Its current director is Donald Zuckerman, who, prior to his current gig, was an independent producer in Los Angeles for years, so he knows what he's talking about when he says, "People have a tendency to say 'hey, we're Colorado, we're beautiful, you know, we've got mountains.' Well, Alberta has mountains and good incentives and Utah has mountains and has a 25 percent incentive…so, there's always someplace you can choose to go…The filmmakers love to go where they can see something different and beautiful but ultimately there has to be an incentive attached to that as well." As of this writing, Colorado's incentives include a cash rebate on qualified expenses and a loan guarantee program for qualifying productions.

The situation becomes less clear-cut with the fact that movies really aren't just movies anymore, and the movie business isn't really strictly about movies. Although we still call it the motion picture industry, it bears scant resemblance to what it was like one hundred years ago—the product isn't even shot on film. Almost all movies are shot digitally or have digital elements in them. So film isn't really film anymore. It's very telling that the Colorado Film Commission has officially expanded its name to the Colorado Office of Film, Television and Media. It now covers a wide array of projects from reality TV to video games. The office has helped to clarify things a bit by defining "film" as "any visual or audiovisual work, including, without limitation, a video game, television show, or a television commercial, that contains a series of related images, regardless of the medium by which the work is fixed and from which it can be viewed or reproduced." That's clear, isn't it?

Most production in the entertainment industry these days isn't for theatrical motion pictures. There are some very prolific reality television production companies in Colorado, including High Noon Entertainment and Citizen Pictures, while the Discovery Channel is bringing thousands of dollars of postproduction work to the state. Then there are video games. Video games have become the most popular entertainment in the world, and their annual sales have now exceeded motion picture box office gross. They're a $52 million industry in Colorado alone.

It was all so much more straightforward in the old days, when the product was film and revenue came from the box office. Now the product is a licensable concept. A movie's profits come from multiple revenue streams: theatrical, television, cable, DVD, the Internet and mobile devices all enter into the picture. When I was a kid, I used to make my own movies using a small consumer camera. At the time, there was no capability of posting them online for the world to see. So in order to show them, I'd stage little neighborhood screenings (that were pretty sparsely attended). Even though I put a lot of production into my little film creations, they were still, in essence, home movies. Nowadays, people can put even the simplest of productions online, and they have the potential to be viewed by millions. So the line can become a little blurry as to whether these are actual "motion pictures" or merely home movies that happen to be viewed by millions of people.

Still, in most people's eyes, feature filmmaking is considered the holy grail of production. And whether or not they can specifically tell you how, everyone knows what a "Hollywood movie" is when they see it. Colorado's Donald Zuckerman is bullish, albeit tentatively so. "We have sites that haven't been filmed in a long time and all things being equal, that's exciting to directors, directors of photography, production designers, producers. You know, but all things have to be equal." And, of course, the great equalizer comes through incentives. "We're looking for business that is real employment for people where the movie or television has a distributor or a good shot at distribution because that's where you get the ancillary benefit of branding Colorado and possibly benefiting tourism in a major way." Sounds a little like "Buck" Buckwalter doesn't it? Today's Zuckerman and Denver's bygone "moving picture man" could be holding a personal conversation with each other across the decades.

We're certainly not seeing a complete exodus of film production out of California. But Colorado is once again finding itself simultaneously on the fringe and at the center of a burgeoning media industry.

Part III

The Past Is Present

Some one hundred years ago, the movies discussed in this book were the height of amusement to an enthusiastic mass market. When viewed by a modern-day audience, most of these films appear stilted and downright primitive, but they have an honesty and directness that cannot be equaled. What we see is the camera capturing the reality before it, without much of the overthought technique common today in even the simplest of productions.

People of today, with every means possible at their disposal, desperately preserve every aspect of their lives for posterity (assuming posterity is even paying attention). Ironically, the people of the early twentieth century, to whom movies were an expensive rarity, weren't so interested in safeguarding their newly created films. Perhaps all of it was so new that they didn't realize the impact these motion pictures would have. Nobody had been able to preserve complete events before. Until that time, people could talk about a past event, write about it, commemorate it with a painting or possibly photograph it. But no one before had been able to resurrect an actual event after the fact, restored in all its moving glory.

Nowadays, we can look at these older films as compelling windows into the past. Sadly, most of the films from those times no longer exist, but it's certainly worth our while to take the opportunity to view the ones that still remain. And since this is a book about films, it would be a very good thing for you to do. Just like a history book that presents an account of a particular war might outline practical steps for visiting famous battlegrounds, this book will tell you how to actually see some of these extraordinary films.

Looking at the Past Today

It's estimated that well over 80 percent of all films from the silent era no longer exist. (I suspect that number is considerably higher for the films that were shot in Colorado.) These films that we now find so precious were already an endangered species even during their heyday. There was no perceived long-term value in movies, and filmmakers saw no reason to preserve their films anymore than you might be inclined to save an expired carton of yogurt. Once the immediate commercial value of a motion picture had been exploited, there was no need for it anymore. Lucky for the film companies, there was good aftermarket value in the films, but not as an evening's entertainment. The silver used in the photographic process could be recovered from the film stock and sold, bringing in a little extra revenue to the margin-conscious filmmakers. Unfortunately, the procedure not only destroyed the films but also any images along with them.

Then there's the matter of the unstable nature of the physical film itself. Until the late 1940s, Hollywood films were distributed on a type of film stock called nitrate film, which is extremely volatile. Not only was there the danger of the film combusting while being projected, but its shelf life was also, as it has turned out, somewhat limited. Over time, these older films began to disintegrate and crumble to dust.

But help has been forthcoming. In 1926, Will Hays, president of the Motion Picture Producers and Distributors of America, called out to the Hollywood studios to offer some of their works to be preserved in a new cold-storage process that had been developed by the Eastman Kodak Company. As Alva Johnston, then writing for the *New York Times*, sardonically put it, "The schoolboys of 3000 or 4000 A.D. may learn about us from the venerable news reels and dramas. Instead of reading corpulent volumes of history, they will troop to the school movie houses to hoot their forefathers and write exercises on 'The Slow Motion Era' and 'Factors That Retarded the Development of the Early Twentieth Century Brain.'"

Despite the sarcasm, the value of preservation was undeniable, and slowly but surely, organizations began forming for the preservation and restoration of our film heritage. Film preservation has been an ongoing concern since then. New York's Museum of Modern Art (MOMA) led the charge, beginning its now famous film collection in 1935. Since that time, the film preservation movement has been growing around the world.

Of course, the best way to view any film is to see it projected on a screen, but with most of the surviving motion pictures from this era, that's a little difficult nowadays. So, it becomes a matter of finding where you can actually watch some of these films. The next-best thing to a live screening is in DVD collections or online, or on the occasional cable television presentation. Bear in mind that with many of the online versions, you have to supply (or imagine) your own musical accompaniment. In the interest of purity, many sources offer the film without a supplementary soundtrack. And it's important to remember that, as they say, the silents were never silent. There was always a musical accompaniment, often sound effects and, as we've seen, sometimes even voiceover actors.

Here, then, is a list of places that have extensive and valuable archives of film, print or photo collections related to the film industry. They're a good source for viewing films or for finding images or other info about the history of films and filmmaking in Colorado, the West and (at least in some cases) beyond. This list is meant to suggest a start for your explorations and is by no means comprehensive.

Library of Congress

This is the granddaddy of all film archives. Quite literally, it's the largest in the world with well over 1 million films and videos housed in its collection. According to the library's own accounting, its moving image collection is housed in "more than 90 miles of shelving for collections storage, 35 climate controlled vaults for sound recording, safety film, and videotape, 124 individual vaults for more flammable nitrate film."

Its collection consists of films that are, in some cases, irreplaceable, including the paper print collection (detailed earlier in this book) consisting of more than three thousand motion pictures, most of them short "actualities" of the early silent era. It represents the only way that we are able to view many of the films from this very early age of moviemaking. Kemp R. Niver, the man who spearheaded the first restoration work, declared, "We are now able to understand how this art form began, evolved, grew, and became the industry it is today."

This is where you can find just about all of the surviving Edison films, including *The Kiss* (1896, listed as the *May Irwin Kiss*—May Irwin being the one doing the kissing) and *The Great Train Robbery* (1903). Also available is a complete print of Gilbert Anderson's 1909 pre–Broncho Billy western, *The Ranchman's Rival*.

And here's how you can access all of the wonderful films in its collection. Regular screenings are presented at the library's Packard Campus. A schedule is available at http://www.loc.gov/avconservation/theater/index.html. General information for the Packard Campus, which houses the collection, is available at http://www.loc.gov/avconservation. You can also go online to view some of the films that have been digitized. Bear in mind that only a small fraction of the library's holdings are available for online viewing, at http://www.loc.gov/rr/mopic/ndlmps.html.

A more comprehensive site, though not quite as user-friendly, is found at the American Memory Collection, at http://memory.loc.gov/ammem/browse/ListSome.php?format=Motion+Picture.

An alphabetical listing of Edison films online at the Library of Congress is at http://memory.loc.gov/ammem/edhtml/edmvalpha.html.

Films from the Library of Congress have appeared in various DVD collections. *Treasures from the American Film Archives* is a five-disc set that includes films from the Library of Congress, as well as other archives. Volume 5 is completely devoted to early western films. Information is available at http://www.filmpreservation.org/dvds-and-books.

Academy of Motion Picture Arts and Sciences

Admit it, when you think of the Academy of Motion Picture Arts and Sciences, you think of the big annual televised Oscar show. But it's so much more than that. The Academy restores, archives and preserves motion pictures—in fact, it's neck-deep in preservation.

The Academy has three locations that are available to the public. The Margaret Herrick Library holds what would be called the physical representations of film—photo stills, graphics, posters, scripts, papers, newspaper clippings and all sorts of hard-to-find memorabilia of films and their makers. Check it out online at http://www.oscars.org/library/index.html.

The Academy Film Archive preserves and houses more than 140,000 film and video items, stored in four climate-controlled vaults. In addition, it hosts regular screenings and events. Learn more about it at http://www.oscars.org/filmarchive/index.html.

The Academy headquarters on Wilshire Boulevard in Los Angeles hosts screenings and exhibits. Take a look at http://www.oscars.org/academy/buildings/headquarters.html.

And the home page for the Academy itself is at http://www.oscars.org.

MOMA

New York's Museum of Modern Art began its film collection in 1935 with a rigorous strategy to collect important films from American and international film producers. It now has one of the most respected collections in the world. It's preserved at the Celeste Bartos Film Preservation Center, whose website is at http://www.moma.org/learn/resources/filmpreservation#historypreservcenter.

The museum holds regular screenings of films of note, details of which you can find at http://www.moma.org/explore/collection/film.

UCLA Film and Television Archive

Based at the University of California–Los Angeles, the UCLA Film and Television Archive houses a collection of films second in size only to the Library of Congress. It was established in 1976 with the union of the libraries of the Academy of Television Arts and Sciences and UCLA's Film Archive. The organization presents an ongoing series of film screenings and events. Information on their activities is available at http://www.cinema.ucla.edu.

History Colorado

History Colorado used to go by the more prosaic name of the Colorado Historical Museum. The museum houses a bounty of western memorabilia, and the library is full of manuscripts, photos and personal files of western subjects. There are no films related to this era of filmmaking, but there is a fantastic collection of photos and personal papers by "Buck" Buckwalter.

The Stephen H. Hart Library can be found at http://www.historycolorado. org/researchers/stephen-h-hart-library-and-research-center. History Colorado's home page is at http://www.historycolorado.org.

Denver Public Library/Western History Collection

The Western History Collection at the Denver Public Library has been aiding authors for decades—from James A. Michener to Willa Cather. Its photo collections cover western subjects from the nineteenth century to the present. It has no films in its archives, but it does hold an entertaining collection of rare stills from films shot in Colorado, primarily those of the Colorado Motion Picture Company. Some photos are available online through its digital collection. You can visit the Western History Collection online at http://history.denverlibrary.org.

History Colorado and the Denver Public Library share access to their digital photo collections at http://digital.denverlibrary.org/cdm.

Niles Essanay Silent Film Museum

As you know from events recounted in this book, the town of Niles, California, is where Broncho Billy Anderson finally set up his West Coast film studio. And the area serves as the location for this small museum, thirty-five miles southeast of San Francisco. Small maybe, but it packs a wallop as far as film screenings, holding silent film showings every Saturday night, along with additional film festivals. It may not have the resources of some of the larger archives listed here, but it makes up for it in dedication. And it has a first-rate collection of very rare photos and film memorabilia—primarily, of course, from the Essanay Company. It is housed in a nickelodeon theater that originally began operations in 1912, the same year that the Essanay Company opened its studio. Connect with them online at http://www.nilesfilmmuseum.org.

Lumière Institute

The Lumière brothers' career in motion pictures was relatively brief but important. If you ever have a chance to see their films onscreen at a local art house or college theater, do so in order to get the full magical effect that the original audiences would have felt—after all, the whole point of their big invention was the presentation of movies as a projected medium.

It seems a long way from the Colorado Rockies to Lyons, France, but that's where the finest collection of Lumière films is housed, in a section of what was once the Lumière photographic factory. It is, as it proclaims on its website, "a museum, a cinema library, a documentation centre, a place for preservation, and a home to memories." And if you want to check out that quote yourself, go to its site at http://institut-lumiere.org.

Southern Methodist University

SMU's Hamon Arts Library in Dallas, Texas, houses a fine collection of pre-nickelodeon films that—in a story that sounds like a movie plot in and of itself—were donated by a private individual from a pile of old nitrate films that had been languishing in a closet for years.

Of particular interest to readers of this book, the collection possesses the only copy of *Tracked by Bloodhounds, or A Lynching at Cripple Creek*—and it's a good copy at that. SMU has made the copy available online at http://digitalcollections.smu.edu/cdm/singleitem/collection/ssm/id/27.

Other early silents are housed in the Sulphur Springs Collection of Pre-nickelodeon Films, at http://digitalcollections.smu.edu/all/cul/ssm. It's a part of the G. William Jones Film and Video Collection, Hamon Arts Library, Southern Methodist University. In fact, it has quite an extensive collection, available online at http://smu.edu/cul/hamon/jones/index.asp.

National Film Preservation Foundation

Finally, if you'd like to get more information on preserving our film heritage, the National Film Preservation Foundation is waiting for you. Check it out at http://www.filmpreservation.org.

Suggested Reading

*T*he following list merely touches the surface of the many resources available for general reading enjoyment. For the more adventurous among you, you can browse through archive editions of the old trade magazines, depending on how well stocked with microfilms your local library is. Many of these are now available in archive collections online. The Moving Picture World *was a trade paper that started publishing in 1907 and ran until 1927.* Photoplay *began publication in 1911 and went through a series of mergers before terminating in 1980. You can get lost in the pages of any of these magazines. Whether that's a good thing or a bad thing, I'll let you decide.*

Balio, Tino. *The American Film Industry*. Revised ed. Madison: University of Wisconsin Press, 1985.

Bowser, Eileen. *The Transformation of Cinema, 1907–1915*. Berkeley: University of California Press, 1994.

Ebert, Roger. *Roger Ebert's Book of Film: From Tolstoy to Tarantino, the Finest Writing from a Century of Film*. New York: W.W. Norton & Company, 1997.

Emrich, David. *Hollywood, Colorado: The Selig Polyscope Company and the Colorado Motion Picture Company*. Lakewood, CO: Post Modern Company, 1997.

Erish, Andrew A. *Col. William N. Selig: The Man Who Invented Hollywood*. Austin: University of Texas Press, 2012.

Kiehn, David. *Broncho Billy and the Essanay Film Company*. Berkeley, CA: Farwell Books, 2003.

Musser, Charles. *The Emergence of Cinema: The American Screen to 1907*. Berkeley: University of California Press, 1994.

———. *Thomas Edison and His Kinetographic Motion Pictures*. New Brunswick, NJ: Rutgers University Press, 1995.

Ramsaye, Terry. *A Million and One Nights*. New York: Simon and Schuster, Inc., 1926. Touchstone edition published in 1986.

Smith, Andrew Brodie. *Shooting Cowboys and Indians*. Boulder: University Press of Colorado, 2003.

Index

V

Vitascope. *See* Edison, Thomas

W

Warner brothers 99
West, Josephine 99
Workers Leaving the Lumière Factory 20

Z

Zoopraxiscope 132
Zuckerman, Donald 142, 143

About the Author

Michael J. Spencer's first motion picture was *Helium!*, a film studying the life of a once-happy balloon gone bad. This short-feature sendup of *The Red Balloon* was chosen to represent the changing face of independent film at the Foundation for Independent Video and Film in New York.

He went on to study film at New York University and UCLA and since then has written and produced a number of award-winning programs for cable and broadcast television. His subjects cover topics as diverse as martial arts to the art of the cocktail, from the frontiers of modern medicine to the culture of tourism.

He divides his time between Colorado and New York.